COLLINS *rambler's guide*

ben nevis & glen coe

The Ramblers

HARVEY

chris townsend

HarperCollins*Publishers*
77–85 Fulham Palace Road
London W6 8JB

The HarperCollins website address is:

www.**fire**and**water**.com

05 04 03 02 01 00

10 9 8 7 6 5 4 3 2 1

First published 2000

Series Editor Richard Sale

We are grateful to the following members of the Ramblers' Association who kindly assisted in checking the walks in this book: Alan Bowley, Andrew Downie, Paul Fannon, Dr P Harrison, Mrs JM Keegan, Ian McAdams, Jackie MacKenzie, Norman Melrose, Bill Ogilvie, Roy Partington, David Poyner, James Riddell, Bobby Robb, Roger A Smith, Francis Spence, Stephen Thomson, Isabel Wilson.

The profiles given for each walk give an indication of the steepness and number of climbs on the route. The times on the profiles are calculated according to the Naismith formula which suggests one hour for each five map kilometres (three map miles) covered, together with an additional 30 minutes for each 300m (1,000ft) of ascent. For most walkers the formula underestimates the time taken for several reasons. Firstly few walkers complete a walk as a route march; secondly, there is no allowance for the terrain crossed, and it is easier to walk quickly over short grass than rough moor; thirdly, there is no allowance for stopping to admire the view, places of interest etc; and finally there is no allowance for rest stops. Rest stops tend to become both longer and more frequent as the walk length increases, so the time error increases as walks get longer. Please check yourself against the times on the first walks you attempt to gauge the time you will take on others.

ISBN 0 00 220115 1

Designed and produced by Drum Enterprises Ltd.
Printed and bound in Great Britain by Scotprint, Musselburgh

CONTENTS

Page No.

INTRODUCTION

The West Highlands are a vast area of steep, rugged mountains cut into by long, winding sea lochs and split by narrow glens. Here are found the highest mountains, biggest cliffs, highest waterfalls and longest valleys in Britain. Ben Nevis and Glen Coe lie in the heart of the region and contain some of the most beautiful and challenging landscapes. The region covered by this guide is bounded by the Great Glen in the north, the West Highland Line and Rannoch Moor in the east, Loch Linnhe in the west and Glen Kinglass and Loch Etive in the south. These boundaries were chosen so that all the walks can be easily reached from either Fort William or Glen Coe. For walkers it's an area of unparalleled variety and the selected walks cover everything from strolls beside seaweed strewn lochs to an ascent of the highest mountain in Britain. In between come wooded gorges, canal banks, waterfalls, narrow rocky ridges, hidden valleys and rushing rivers, a wonderful mix of every type of scenery and feature. There are thirty walks in the book but they are only an introduction to a complex area that merits much exploration.

GEOLOGY & GEOGRAPHY

Like the rest of the Highlands the hills of Ben Nevis and Glen Coe are the dissected remnants of an ancient plateau and hence are similar in height. Before this plateau was formed seabed sediments were forced upwards as high as the Himalayas some four hundred million years ago, becoming metamorphosed into schists and quartzites under the great pressures involved. These pressures also folded the mountains into a north-east to south-west pattern that still forms the grain of the land today and which can be clearly seen in the Great Glen and its continuation in Loch Linnhe, and also in the line of Glen Etive. Volcanic eruptions burst through the rocks in places leaving extrusions of granite, rhyolite and other rocks that now form the bulk of Ben Nevis and the hills on either side of Glen Coe. The other mountains in the area are mostly built of metamorphic rock though there are some other intrusions of volcanic rocks in places such as the granite Trilleachan Slabs in Glen Etive.

The particular form of volcanic activity that formed the Ben Nevis and Glen Coe hills is known as cauldron subsidence. This occurred when the deep beds of lava that had spread over the metamorphic rocks were split by circular ring faults some five or six miles across. The huge round blocks formed by these faults then sank, to be replaced by liquid magma boiling up from below and from volcanoes on the rim. The rocks, mostly granite and rhyolite, formed by this magma were protected inside the cauldron from the erosion that removed the surrounding lava and now form the mountains we know today. The Glen Coe ring fault is actually oval in shape, measuring some 5 × 9 miles (8 × 14.5km). The hard volcanic rocks created by cauldron subsidence form great cliffs and are very good for rock climbing.

After all this activity the land subsided almost to sea level to form a flat plain which, around 20–30 million years ago, rose to become the vast plateau mentioned above. Rivers cut into this plateau to form the current pattern of glens and long hill ridges.

These complicated processes took place over unimaginable periods of geological time of course. Much more recently a series of ice ages, the last of which only ended some 10,000 years ago, carved the landforms familiar today. The scale of the ice was enormous. During the earliest period it was 4920ft (1,500m) thick. The slow movement of glaciers formed the scenery so typical of the region, scouring out deep loch beds, slicing off the ends of ridges to form truncated spurs, fining down ridges to long thin aretes and cutting the U-shaped glens with hanging valleys high on their sides that are so typical of the region.

HISTORY

People have lived in the Highlands for 8,000 years or so, and there are still some signs of the earliest inhabitants in the form of chambered cairns, standing stones, stone circles and other megalithic buildings though few of these lie in the Ben Nevis and Glen Coe regions. The first stone age people were few in number and with their crude stone implements had little impact on the environment. It was the introduction of iron by the Celts, who started colonising the Highlands around 700 BC, that started to change the landscape. With tools such as axes they could begin clearing the vast forests that covered the land and with ploughs they could cultivate lowland areas.

The first Celtic immigrants became known as the Picts. The Scots, who colonised Scotland from Ireland from the 5th century AD onwards, were also a Celtic people. Initially the Picts were followers of the ancient pre-Christian religion while the Scots were Christians. Missionary work by the latter, culminating with St Columba who arrived on Iona in 563 AD and his disciples such as St Mundus who lived for a time on an island in Loch Leven near the foot of Glen Coe, eventually converted all the Picts.

The Scots and Picts were united politically under one king

in 843 AD after the Picts, whose kingdom lay in the north and west, had been weakened by decades of warfare with Viking raiders. For a time the Vikings not only ruled the Hebrides, Shetland and Orkney but also the northernmost mainland and most of what is now Argyll. There are many legends of the wars with the Vikings, often involving the great Celtic hero Fingal (see Walk 12 for one story).

The Scots were organised into large family groups or tribes, the famous clans. In the Ben Nevis and Glen Coe areas the people lived by subsistence farming, with black cattle as the main source of wealth, though sheep were also kept, and fish caught in the sea lochs. However by the 1500s the gap between the richer clans of the more fertile lowlands to the south and the Highlanders was growing and some of the Highland clans, most notably the MacDonalds of Glen Coe, took to raiding neighbouring lands, both Lowland and Highland, and stealing cattle which were often spirited away into Coire Gabhail (see Walk 24). These raids made them unpopular with their fellow clans while their armed support for the Royalists in the Civil War and then the opponents of William of Orange made the authorities regard them as a problem. Thus was the stage set for the infamous Massacre of Glencoe (see Walk 5) in 1692.

At the same time as the clans were raiding and feuding, cattle droving became important with regular drives to markets in the Lowlands and in England. Some of today's hill paths and tracks follow the routes of the old drove roads. Proper roads as opposed to hill paths didn't exist until after the first Jacobite rising in 1715 when it was deemed necessary to have them for the quick movement of troops. The first were built in the years after 1724 by General George Wade and are often called Wade's Roads. The name is also applied inaccurately to many roads built by his successors, especially General Caulfield who increased the road network greatly after the defeat of the '45 Rising at Culloden. One of his roads, that from Stirling to Fort William, passes through the region covered by this book and sections of it are included in some of the walks.

The failure of the '45 Rising was one of the main causes of the end of the clan system. Initially property had been held communally by the clan and the people selected the chief. By the 1600s however the post was hereditary and the chief owned the land and was paid rent by the clan members. After Culloden the military power of the chiefs was broken and they could no longer raise bodies of armed men. They still claimed ownership of clan lands however. Men were now of no value to them but money was needed for their new roles as members of the aristocracy. At first they obtained this by increasing rents to exorbitant levels and by cattle droving. The former forced thousands of Highlanders to emigrate. Droving expanded massively in the mid 1700s and remained important for a hundred years until steamers and trains took over.

'The Coming of the Sheep', though, was the real cause of major change. In the south the demand for wool was growing and sheep were becoming of great value, so the clan chiefs either sold the land to sheep farmers from the south or brought in sheep of their own. Mass production was the way to make money so farms were combined. Large sheep farms required fewer workers so many men were superfluous. The chiefs had no need of their people now nor any remaining loyalty to them. The result was the notorious Clearances.

The environment suffered too. At the beginning of the eighteenth century much of the great Wood of Caledon still remained but after the 1715 Rising had been crushed, felling increased to feed the iron-smelters in the south and to put money in the pockets of the landowners. By 1813 when coke replaced charcoal in furnaces much of the forest was gone. It could still have recovered however but for the sheep. Sheep are extremely destructive animals, cropping vegetation almost to ground level and preventing the regeneration of shrubs and trees. 'Hooved locusts' the great Scottish conservation pioneer John Muir called them after seeing their depredations in the Sierra Nevada mountains of California.

Although sheep remain on the hills, after 1850 they were replaced by deer in many areas as the sporting estate was born. The deer also prevented the return of the forest as numbers boomed, mainly due to the lack of natural predators. These had gone with the forests: the last wolf is said to have been killed in 1743. Sporting estates still make up most of the land in the Highlands, preventing the return of people, wildlife and trees. The last century has seen the arrival of hydroelectric dams, regimented conifer plantations, ski resorts and other developments, some of them arguably beneficial, some clearly destructive. None however have the effect that continued over-grazing by sheep and deer have.

At the same time as the sporting estates arose so did the pursuit of mountaineering and hillwalking. This was aided by new roads and railways such as the West Highland Line to Fort William, which opened in 1894. Perhaps though the key event for the modern walker was the publication in 1891 of Sir Hugh Munro's *Tables of Heights over 3000ft* in the Scottish Mountaineering Club Journal, listing all the hills in Scotland over 3,000ft (915m). Climbing all these summits, known as Munros, is a popular pastime.

NATURAL HISTORY
Flora

The loss of the forest that once cloaked the glens and the lower slopes of the hills has had a great effect on the natural history of the area. The acid soils that cover much of the poorly drained land in the glens and on the lower slopes of the hills make for large areas of blanket bog, especially as overgrazing by sheep and deer continues. 'A devastated terrain' and a 'wet desert' are two descriptions. The National Trust for Scotland, who could do much more to allow regeneration of trees on their Glen Coe and Dalness estates (or much less, reducing sheep and deer numbers drastically is all that's needed), admit that 'the scarcity of trees and shelter accounts for the lack of animal numbers.'

That said, there is still much to see in the area. Tiny fragments of the Caledonian Forest still exist in places. Magnificent towering Scots pine can be found along with graceful birches, delicate rowans and, more rarely, pale-barked aspens and bulky dark-leaved oaks. Beside the slower, wider rivers alders and willows grow. The Glen Nevis gorge (see Walk 2) holds one of the finest remnants of forest, its steep flanks, out of reach of sheep and deer, packed with a riotous wealth of wonderful trees. Other groves of native trees can be found further down the glen, standing out against the blocks of commercial conifers. Elsewhere there are small fenced areas where the forest is slowly returning (there's one in upper Glen Etive) while scatterings of birches and rowans grow in many steep-sided gorges, again out of reach of browsing animals. The thin green lines running up the hillsides show what the land round about could be like. There are patches of native woodland alongside Loch Etive too (see Walk 7) and above Loch Leven (see Walk 4). These woodlands are marvellous at any time of the year but are especially attractive in spring when the pale new leaves slowly unfurl bringing warmth and colour after the drab grey of winter and again in autumn when the leaves turn bright gold and orange and the rowan berries glow red.

Other than bracken, whose pale green curled fronds look attractive in spring but which quickly become dense, high, fly-ridden dark green thickets before fading into golden brown with the coming of autumn, there are few plants of any height outside the forest. Coarse grasses – matgrass, tufted hair-grass and deer-grass – make up the bulk of the moorland vegetation along with large areas of sphagnum moss. On drier slopes and tussocks ling, bell heather and cross-leaved heath grow, giving, in summer, the purple sheen the Highlands are famous for.

In the boggiest areas the nodding fluffy white flowers of bog cotton (or cotton grass), the yellow spikes of bog asphodel and the shrubby sweet-scented bog myrtle are common. In places the purple flowers of the insect-eating common butterwort rise from a flat rosette of sticky leaves. The pretty little four-petalled yellow tormentil dots dry areas along with tiny white-flowered heath bedstraw and the larger unfortunately named but still attractive lousewort, also with white flowers. Many other flowers can be found by the keen botanist; wood anemone, wild hyacinth, bluebell, violets, celandine and various orchids are all present in places. Burns are good places for flowers and from low down to high in the hills may be lined with miniature, easily missed flowers such as alpine lady's mantle, alpine meadow rue and mountain everlasting. More noticeable and attractive are the bright stars of the yellow and purple saxifrages.

High on the mountain slopes crowberry and blaeberry, with its delicious purple finger-staining berries, appear along with more saxifrages and other alpine flowers such as fleshy rose-root and dwarf cornel. Higher still and mats of tiny plants fall underfoot, most of them unnoticeable to all but the keen botanist. Some stand out though, in particular the mats of pink moss campion. The creeping woody stems of dwarf willow can be found here too.

Fauna

The only large wild land mammal left is the red deer and herds of these, some hundreds strong, can be seen on the hills year round. In summer the thick greyish winter coat gives way to the brighter red-brown one that gives the deer its name. In autumn the glens and corries echo with the wild roaring of the rutting stags, a thrilling sound. Year round you will hear the short sharp bark given by hinds to warn of your approach and then watch as the deer flow away over the hillside. The much smaller roe deer lives in forested areas but is rarely seen. Tracks in the snow are the most common sign of them. Most other mammals are shy too. In open country only mountain hares, which turn white in winter, on the tops and brown hares in the glens are likely to be seen. Careful observation may pick up a grey hill fox trotting across the hillside but these animals are amazingly well camouflaged. Wild cats are present but being nocturnal are hardly ever seen. Stoats and weasels frequent lower areas and may be seen darting through the grass. The former are more easily observed in winter when their coats turn white. In the forests red squirrels may chatter at you from branches but their main predator, the sleek pine marten, is much harder to see. Otters live in the rivers but again are secretive. In all my wanderings I've only seen one. In the sea lochs grey seals are often seen basking on rocks or swimming.

Birds are far more visible and it would be a poor walk when few were seen or heard. Red grouse exploding out of the heather or peat with their harsh guttural cry often startle walkers while high above buzzards soar, their mewing call a feature of the hills. Occasionally a larger circling bird may be seen, the magnificent golden eagle. Ravens are well worth watching as they are one of the most impressive fliers, diving and swerving round the crags. Hooded crows are common and regularly seen in the glens.

Despite the harsh environment a surprising number of birds live on the mountaintops. The most typical one is the ptarmigan, whose grey summer plumage blends in so well with the stony ground that you can be only a few steps away and not see one until it moves. In winter they turn white, which makes them stand out unless there is good snow cover. The guttural cry is often heard before the birds are seen. Just as well camouflaged, but rarer and far less often seen, is the dotterel, an attractive small plover. Small birds are less common though meadow pipits dot the lower hillsides, so undistinguished in their brown plumage as to be almost unnoticeable. Higher up the more attractive black and white snow buntings are often seen.

Lochs, both fresh and salt, are good places for birds. On the higher lochans black-throated and red-throated divers may be found. Their wild manic cry can be quite disturbing when heard in the dark from a high camp. On lower waters grey herons stand motionless on one leg in the marshes, watching for prey, or flap slowly over the reed beds or salt flats while stately white mute swans drift along the lochs. Ungainly looking cormorants spread their wings out as they perch on stumps of driftwood in the sea lochs then dive sleekly to resurface surprising distances away. Common sandpipers bob up and down from lochside rocks then call plaintively as they dart away. In the burns stumpy dippers fly just above the water, their short wings a blur. Lapwing, curlew and oystercatcher whirl and call above the shores of Loch Etive or Loch Leven.

There are a host of other birds to be seen and the walker interested in them and other wildlife will find a pair of binoculars invaluable. There are many lightweight pairs available. The 8x21 ones I take hillwalking weigh just 5.5oz (150g) and fit easily into a jacket pocket.

ACCESS

There is a long-established *de facto* right to roam in the Scottish hills which has a strong legal basis. It is expected that the Scottish Parliament will shortly enshrine this tradition in new access legislation. This will guarantee freedom of access for informal recreation to most of Scotland's countryside, providing this is exercised responsibly, taking due account of conservation and management needs.

Access legislation is part of the Scottish Government's land reform programme. This also includes proposals to establish national parks and 'right to buy' arrangements for local communities and crofters. These measures, which are long overdue, will help to prevent further decline in the Highland environment, including its enjoyment by the public, as estates are bought and sold by anyone with enough money. The first national parks will be established in Loch Lomond and the Trossachs and in the Cairngorms. A national park covering the Ben Nevis and Glencoe area may follow at a later stage.

Generally, outside of the deer-stalking season, most landowners don't object to walkers wandering where they will. During stag stalking (mid-August to mid-October or part thereof) most private estates like walkers to enquire about where and when stalking is taking place and plan walks to avoid these areas. Telephone numbers of factors and keepers plus maps of estates can be found in the regularly updated book *Heading for the Scottish Hills*, produced jointly by the Scottish Landowners Federation (SLF) and the Mountaineering Council of Scotland (MCofS). There is also a Hillphones scheme, organised by the MCofS and Scottish Natural Heritage (SNH), whereby recorded information about stalking on some estates is available from August to October. Of the area covered by this book, the Grey Corries and Mamores are covered by the Hillphones scheme. The number to call at the time of writing is 01855 831511. There are no restraints on access on the Glen Coe and Dalness estates owned by the National Trust for Scotland (NTS) and walks on Forestry Commission land are open year round unless felling is taking place nearby.

Not all estates are listed in *Heading for the Scottish Hills* never mind part of the Hillphones scheme. Even when there is a phone number to ring the information given may be unhelpful. Being treated with hostility and told walkers aren't wanted on the hills at all, as I have been (not I hasten to add by any estate covered by this book), isn't much use in helping plan a day out. My response when this occurs or when no information is available is to go anyway.

DOGS

Dogs taken on the hills must be kept under control and not allowed to chase animals, whether wild or domestic. During lambing season, from March to May, they should be left at home as even the presence of a well-behaved dog can upset pregnant sheep.

MOUNTAIN BIKES
Mountain bikes can be useful for long approaches to the hills. Their use on vehicle tracks is fine but on paths and off-road they can cause great erosion, especially when the ground is wet.

Freedom of access should be exercised with care. When crossing cultivated land try to use paths or tracks or field margins. Use gates whenever possible but where walls or fences have to be crossed, do so carefully to avoid damage to the structure.

Further guidance on using the countryside responsibly should be available in the Scottish Outdoor Access Code. This is expected to accompany the right of access when it is approved by the Scottish Parliament. The aim of the proposed Code is to show how recreational users, land managers and public bodies can help each other to make sure the right of access works well on the ground.

THE WALKER AND THE ENVIRONMENT
Path Erosion
Walking in the hills is an increasingly popular pastime and the Ben Nevis and Glen Coe area is one of the most visited in the Highlands. In general the impact of walkers on the landscape is small. However path erosion is a growing problem, especially on the often boggy and therefore easily eroded approaches to the hills. Path repairs have been carried out in many areas and are needed in many others. This is an expensive and sometimes intrusive remedy however. Whilst sheer numbers alone can cause erosion, much damage to paths is the result of bad walking practices.

Minimising Path Erosion
The main way to reduce damage to paths is to stay on them, preferably in the centre. Walking on the edges breaks these down and widens the path, leading to a spreading, unsightly scar. Even when paths are wet and muddy you should stay on them. If you're concerned about wet feet, wear gaiters and proof your boots well. Even then, keeping your feet dry may be impossible in wet conditions. Outside of winter conditions, I wear lightweight footwear that dries quickly and just accept that my feett will get wet.

A common cause of erosion on steep hillsides is where people have cut the corners of zigzags, creating a channel down which water can run. Although it's very tempting to do this, especially in descent, it's important to stay on the path.

Walking Off Paths
Where there are no paths care should be taken to leave as little trace of your passing as possible. Rocks, gravel and other hard surfaces are more resistant to wear than soft, wet ground. Dry grass or heather covered slopes stand up to impact better than boggy areas.

Cairns

Marking cross country routes with cairns detracts from the feeling of being in wild country and can also lead to paths appearing where there were none before as other walkers follow them. There are far too many cairns on established paths too, so many indeed that they can cause confusion rather than help with route finding. I often knock down cairns and never build them. Summit cairns and cairns on prominent points, many of which are very old and have cultural and historical associations, are another matter and should be left alone. Cairns covered with lichen or moss are a sign of antiquity as are ones that have been carefully constructed rather than just piled up. With new cairns the holes the stones were prised from may still be visible. If so the stones should be replaced as far as possible.

Camping

Camping in wild country is a wonderful experience. It can cause damage if done carelessly however. The aim of all wild campers should be to leave no trace of their presence. With modern lightweight equipment this isn't difficult.

Two practices that aren't necessary if you know how to choose a good site and how to pitch your tent properly are using rocks to hold down tent pegs and digging drainage trenches round a tent. I camp in the hills regularly and never do either of these. Rocks on pegs is by far the commoner of the two practices and I have all too often spent time dismantling unsightly rings of stones left by other campers. If you do ever put rocks on tent pegs or decide to move those left by others, either replace the rocks in their original holes, if these can be seen, or else spread them out over a rocky or vegetation free area or even dump them in the nearest stream.

Campers should always use stoves. Campfires damage the ground and leave long-lasting scars as well as being inefficient.

Safety

The Lochaber area is characterised by high steep mountains divided by deep, rugged glens. For walkers this means rough, difficult terrain where progress can be slow. It also means that it can be a long way, in time if not in distance, from the nearest road or habitation. For example, the main road through Glen Coe may be visible from much of the Aonach Eagach but getting down to it is another matter. This area is also one of the wettest in Britain and the higher you go, the wetter it gets. Fort William has a mean annual rainfall of 77in (200cm), quite high in itself, but on the summit of Ben Nevis, just 4 miles (6.4km) away, the mean annual rainfall is double

LITTER
All rubbish should be taken home. This includes orange peel and other biodegradable material as this can attract scavenging birds such as crows and gulls into the hills where they may then devastate local bird populations by eating the young and eggs. Removing other people's litter is good practice. Carrying a small plastic bag for this is worthwhile. Some rubbish is most unusual. On a family outing we once removed an American flag on a stick from the top of the Coire Gabhail gorge. Unfortunately the culprits had also left a half-burnt sticky mess of melted plastic, congealed foil and rotting food which it was quite unpleasant to remove. Burning rubbish is just not acceptable. Aside from the likelihood that it won't all be consumed the fire itself will leave a scar and could get out of control.

TOILETS

There is nothing more sordid than seeing pink and white strands of used toilet paper sticking out from a pile of faeces lying in the grass or half-hidden under a rock. As well as being unpleasant to see, the unthinking disposal of human waste can pollute water supplies and cause illness. Ideally, toilets should be sited at least 200 yards (183m) from the nearest water. Where this isn't possible due to the prevalence of tiny streams and boggy pools, head uphill and away from the main watercourses. You should keep well away from any paths or obvious walking routes such as ridge crests too. Unless there is a risk of fire toilet paper should be burnt. A lighter or box of matches can be carried in the plastic bag with the paper for this purpose. Faeces should be covered by stones or loose vegetation or, even better, buried. Small plastic or metal lightweight trowels are available for this. When carried, an ice axe makes a good trenching tool. In soft soil the heel of a boot can be used. The hole doesn't need to be deep. Indeed, decomposition takes place more quickly near the surface so 4–6in (10–15cm) is fine.

that at 157in (400cm). Add in strong winds and thick mist and conditions on the hills can be severe even in summer. In winter snow and ice can make walking on the high tops both difficult and dangerous.

This is not to say that walking on these hills is a risky pastime. Only a very tiny minority of walkers ever gets into difficulties. Sensible preparation is needed however for walks which take you beyond waymarked forest and glen footpaths. Being able to navigate accurately with map and compass is essential. Adequate footwear is very important as most accidents in the hills are caused by simple slips. Wellingtons may be fine for muddy forest trails but once you venture higher then proper walking boots or shoes are needed. A small rucksack should always be carried, containing at the minimum a waterproof jacket and trousers (if not worn), spare sweater, hat and gloves, food and drink, small first aid kit, safety whistle, map and compass. For longer walks a plastic survival bag and a torch (with spare batteries) are also recommended. An ice axe and crampons, and the skill to use them, are required in winter conditions for walks above glen level. The short daylight hours of winter need taking into account too.

Mountain Rescue

Two highly experienced mountain rescue teams cover the walks described in this book, the Lochaber and Glen Coe teams. These teams are voluntary bodies and rely on donations for funding. Collecting boxes can be found in outdoor shops, cafes, bars and other places throughout the area. Please contribute if you can.

If an accident occurs priority must be given to ensuring the safety of those not involved before giving first aid to the injured. This means ensuring that people keep warm and dry and aren't somewhere exposed to danger from avalanches or rockfall or perched precariously above steep drops. To call for help use the standard distress call of six blasts of a whistle or flashes of a torch repeated at intervals of a minute. If possible someone should go for help.

If you have a mobile phone this should of course be used if it will work. However there is no coverage in many areas of the Highlands and even where there is, phones may not work in gullies, below cliffs or in other sheltered areas. This means you may have to climb high up a hillside to get a signal, which may not be advisable or even feasible in poor weather. Mobile phones should only be used if there is genuine need. If you can get yourself and your party safely off the hill this should be done. A phone is not a substitute for having the necessary skills and equipment.

To call out a rescue team dial 999 and ask for the police. You should have the following information to give them: the exact location of the incident with six figure grid reference and a description of any obvious features, the time the incident occurred, the number of casualties, a brief outline of what happened, the nature and severity of the injuries and any treatment given. This should be written down to avoid mistakes. A pencil stub and some notepaper can be kept in the first aid kit for this.

Someone should stay with the injured person if possible. If they have to be left alone then the location should be marked with something bright or reflective that can quickly be spotted.

Midges, Ticks and Clegs

Midges (*Culicoides impunctatus*) are tiny biting insects that can make life miserable, unbearable even, on warm, humid days when they attack in swarms. They are a particular problem for campers. Luckily, midges can't fly in more than a light breeze and don't like heavy rain or hot sun. Calm cloudy days, especially at dawn and dusk, bring them out in their millions however. Insect repellents will stop them biting, though they still crawl maddeningly over your skin. Citronella products are not so good. Long sleeved, tightly woven clothing is also useful in protecting against midges while headnets may be essential for the sanity of campers.

Ticks are very small insects that live in rough vegetation and bracken and can attach themselves to you or your clothing when you brush past. They then insert their mouthparts into your flesh and suck up blood, swelling as they fill. They're not the immediate irritation midges are but the bites can transmit disease. As ticks don't bite immediately a body search at the end of the day can often locate and remove them before they've broken the skin. When a tick is embedded in the flesh it needs to be removed very carefully so the mouthpiece doesn't break off and remain in the wound. A pair of tweezers is useful for this. Dabbing them with alcohol, petrol or insect repellent can encourage them to withdraw. When walking through long vegetation tucking trousers into socks and perhaps dabbing the ankles with insect repellent is a good way to prevent ticks attaching themselves. Ticks are a particular problem in early summer.

Clegs (*Haematopota* sp) are large buzzing flies that can inflict a painful bite. In humid weather they can be extremely irritating as they will follow you for long periods of time, trying to land on any exposed flesh. If you stop to try and swat them they usually stop too. Repellent can stop them biting though not flying round your head. Bites can swell into itchy lumps.

LYME DISEASE
The Ramblers' Association Factsheet 15 provides information on the above which is caused by tick bites. Although treatable, Lyme Disease can be serious if the symptoms are not properly diagnosed. For more details contact The Ramblers for a copy of the factsheet or visit their website at www.ramblers.org.uk

THE CALEDONIAN CANAL

/ ❖ 🌳 ⚜ 🏰 🌲

START/FINISH:
Banavie on the A830 Mallaig road, 2½ miles (4km) from Fort William. The regular number 45 bus service from Fort William to Corpach can drop you at Banavie. There is also a large car park just off the main road. Please note that if you decide to continue to Gairlochy you commit yourself to walking back to Banavie as there is no public transport link between Gairlochy and Banavie

DISTANCE:
12½ miles (20km) for the full walk, 4 miles (6km) for the shortest option

APPROXIMATE TIME:
1½–5/6 hours

HIGHEST POINT: 492ft (150m)

MAPS: OS Landranger 41 Ben Nevis, Fort William and surrounding area

REFRESHMENTS:
Cafés and bars in Corpach, Moorings Hotel in Banavie

ADVICE:
A good all-year round walk

Winding through lush countryside with a backdrop of big mountains the Caledonian Canal is a quiet waterway in a remote setting. The walking along the towpath is easy and gives superb views of Ben Nevis and surrounding hills. Closer to hand the rich woodlands along the banks, the architectural details of the canal and the boats on the water add interest to the walk.

A   Banavie 111 770

Banavie is on the edge of the town of Corpach. Corpach means the Place of Bodies as it was here that ships waited in the distant past to take the corpses of the powerful, which had been carried through the Great Glen, sometimes all the way from Inverness, down Loch Linnhe for burial on the sacred island of Iona.

a   A set of locks known as Neptune's Staircase lies next to the car park. The walk starts on the far side of the locks and follows the east bank of the canal.

B   Neptune's Staircase 113 770

Neptune's Staircase consists of an impressive set of eight locks that raise the level of the canal 64ft (19.2m) in a distance of just 550 yards (500m). Most of the lock gates are made of cast iron covered with pine, oak being too costly due to the demands of the Royal Navy for wood for ships for the Napoleonic Wars. Even so, this great engineering achievement cost £50,000, a huge sum for the time. On the west bank of the canal can be seen the old lockkeepers' houses, now private dwellings, which have large bow windows to allow clear vision up and down the canal. Neptune's Staircase takes the canal from sea level into the Great Glen. A mile (1.6km) to the south-west the canal reaches the sea at Loch Linnhe.

C   Mountain View

There is a superb view of the great cliff buttressed bulk of Ben Nevis from the canal just beyond Neptune's Staircase with beyond it the more elegant looking peaks of Carn Mor Dearg, Aonach Mor and the Grey Corries.

b The towpath leaves the last buildings behind and there is suddenly a feeling of solitude as the canal runs between dense rows of trees fronted by dense thickets of hawthorn and brambles. Through the deciduous woodland to the east there are glimpses down to the river Lochy, the natural waterway of this part of the Great Glen.

The Caledonian Canal near Gairlochy

c After a couple of miles the canal runs on an embankment high above the woods. The river makes a loop to the east here, round a small hillock on which stand the remains of Torcastle, which is associated with Banquo of Macbeth fame. There are some rich deciduous woodlands here with paths through them and it's worth taking the short diversion to wander under the great beeches and other trees, especially in the spring when flowers brighten the forest floor or in autumn when the leaves are turning gold and red. There are some cottages by the canal here too. Access to these is via tunnels under the canal that also carry the Allt Sheangain on its way to the Lochy. If this is as far as you want to go then this is the way to access

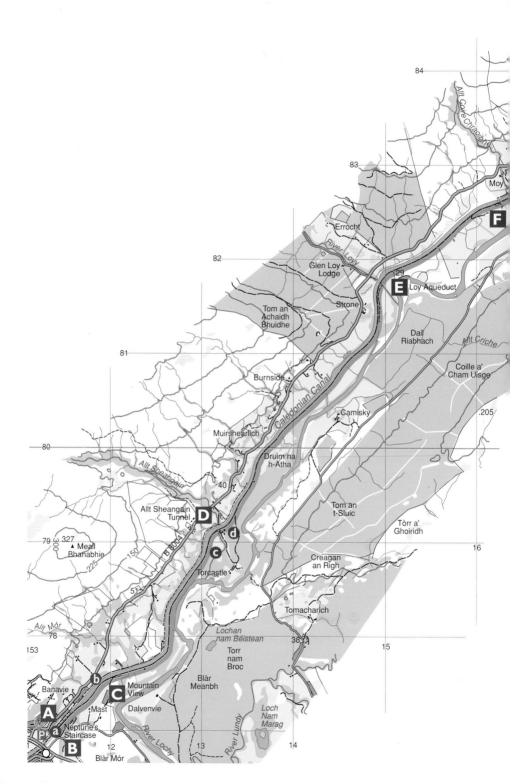

the road on the far side of the canal, along which you can walk back to Banavie. Finding the tunnel is not that easy however as the narrow path down to it isn't marked. The first time I came this way I met a party of rather annoyed American walkers searching for the tunnel so they could return to Gairlochy along the road. Their guidebook simply said the tunnel was below the canal by the cottages. They'd tried a number of tracks but not found it. The key is a telegraph pole with a small metal plate with the number 837 on it as the path goes down the bank directly behind this. The tunnel is right next to the path. It's used by vehicles for access to the houses on this side of the canal so watch out for these when walking through it. Once through the tunnel a track leads up to the B8004. There is a restaurant and phone box here.

D The Allt Sheangain Tunnel
Even if you're not returning from here it's worth going down the path to see the tunnels. There are three equal sized arches, their brickwork now mossy and green. Two of them carry the shallow waters of the stream; the third is cobbled and used for farm and other vehicles as well as walkers. On the far side of the tunnel there is a small weir in the stream to help control spates.

d For those continuing the pleasant towpath walking leads on to Gairlochy. This is the end of this section of the canal as it joins Loch Lochy here.

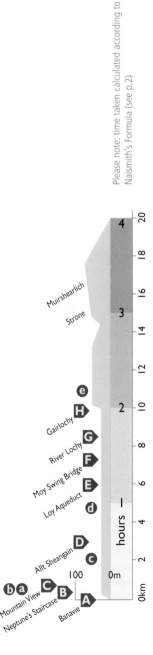

Please note: time taken calculated according to Naismith's Formula (see p.2)

JAMES WATT first proposed the Caledonian Canal in 1773 but work didn't start until 1803. The canal was built by the famous Scottish civil engineer Thomas Telford. It opened in 1822 and for the first time boats could go from the Irish to the North Sea without having to go round the stormswept north coast of Scotland.

The canal runs along the Great Glen linking Loch Linnhe in the west with the Moray Firth in the east.

The Great Glen is the obvious line for a coast to coast link as it is a geological fault line that splits the Highlands in two with a highpoint of just 115ft (35m). Much of the fault is filled with water and although it is 60½ miles (97km) from salt water to salt water only 22 miles (35km) of this consists of the canal. The rest is made up of Lochs Lochy, Oich and Ness.

E   The Loy Aqueduct

Here the canal crosses the River Loy on a large aqueduct. On the return walk along the B8004 a track by the road bridge leads down to a view of the aqueduct with its big central arch under which the river runs and smaller side ones for use by vehicles and farm animals. Glen Loy has one claim to fame for it was down the glen that Bonnie Prince Charlie marched with his growing army in 1745 after raising his standard at Glenfinnan.

F   The Moy Swing Bridge

The old swing bridge here, still in working order, is made of cast iron.

G   River Lochy

As you approach Gairlochy views open up across the River Lochy which here runs across wide stony shallows with many gravel banks. Rolling hills make up the horizon beyond the river.

Loch Lochy from Gairlochy

H   Gairlochy

The Allt Sheangain Tunnel

Gairlochy is a set of double locks where the canal reaches Loch Lochy. There is a swing-bridge and Thomas Telford also had a house here, which still stands next to the locks.

e   To return to Banavie cross the canal and take the B8004. While the walk along the canal towpath affords superb views of Ben Nevis and its surrounding mountains, the road runs higher up the side of the glen and as it climbs the views become more and more panoramic and spectacular. Watch out for cars on the narrow road. If it is really busy, as it can be at the height of the summer season, you could walk back along the towpath. The sights to be seen from the road should not be missed however, and the walk might be best done out of season when there is less traffic on the road – especially at weekends.

THE NEVIS GORGE AND STEALL FALLS

This short, easy walk climbs through a wild steep-sided wooded gorge to upper Glen Nevis and Steall waterfall, one of the finest falls in the Highlands.

START/FINISH:
End of Glen Nevis road. There is a summer bus service from Fort William to the Lower Falls in Glen Nevis, just over a mile (1.6km) from the road end

DISTANCE:
2½ miles (4km)
(5 miles and 8km if walking from Lower Falls)

APPROXIMATE TIME:
1½–3 hours

HIGHEST POINT:
738ft (225m) in upper Glen Nevis

MAPS:
Harveys Walker's Map or Superwalker Ben Nevis; OS Outdoor Leisure 38 Ben Nevis & Glen Coe; OS Landranger 41 Ben Nevis, Fort William and surrounding area

REFRESHMENTS:
Cafes in lower Glen Nevis, all services in Fort William

ADVICE:
Spring and autumn are recommended seasons for this walk due to the colours of the woodland foliage

Steall Falls

A Glen Nevis road end 167 691

Glen Nevis is one of the best known and most impressive glens in the Highlands. A single-track road runs for 2 miles (3.2km) up the increasingly narrow and mountainous glen from Fort William. At the road end there is a parking area and a number of information notices. Ben Nevis walls the glen to the north and there are dozens of other mountains that can be climbed from the glen (see Walks 18, 19, 20 & 30). Immediately above the car park to the north the Allt Coire Eoghainn pours down in a 1,230ft (375m) long waterslide from high up on Ben Nevis. To the east the steep rocky crags of Meall Cumhann apparently block the way though a close look shows a slight notch in the steep mountainside. This is the Glen Nevis Gorge.

GLEN NEVIS
In the past Glen Nevis had a reputation as an evil place. In *Highways and Byways in the West Highlands* Seton Gordon quotes a saying that it's 'a glen on which God has turned His Back'.

View down Glen Nevis from the Nevis Gorge

B Glen Nevis Lower Falls 145 684

A mile or so (1.6km) before the end of the road a bridge crosses the Water of Nevis. There is a bus service to this point and a car park and the walk can be started here with a stroll along the winding road to its end. Directly above the bridge the Lower Falls of Glen Nevis tumble some 40ft (12m) down a rocky section of the glen, the crashing waters split in two by

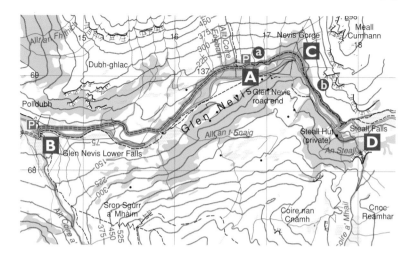

a large boulder. Dominating the scene is the pale quartzite cone of Sgurr a'Mhaim, the second highest summit of the Mamores range. Because of its prominence it's often mistaken for Ben Nevis, which in fact lies to the north but which is too massive for it to be seen clearly from so close by. The lower wooded slopes of Ben Nevis are covered with small crags here. This area, called Polldubh, is very popular with rock climbers.

a   From the road end a path, signposted for Corrour Station, sets off east into the trees. Very soon it turns south-east and starts to climb into the steep, rocky mouth of the narrow gorge, staying well above the river. As it twists its way across the side of the gorge the path crosses some open areas where there is a bit of a drop and care should be taken, especially if the ground is icy or slippery with mud.

C   The Nevis Gorge 173 691

The Nevis Gorge lies where the Water of Nevis is squeezed between two great rocky spurs jutting out from Ben Nevis to the north and Sgurr a'Mhaim to the south. A thick, magnificent forest of oak, birch, rowan, aspen and Scots pine covers the slopes of the gorge with towering crags rising above and the white water of the river crashing over massive boulders below, a scene 'Himalayan in character' in W.H.Murray's oft-quoted description. From the v-shaped mouth of the gorge a distant white slash can be seen through the trees. This is our destination, Steall Falls. Looking back from the path, which in places is carved out of the rock, there is a fine view down Glen Nevis.

The Nevis Gorge

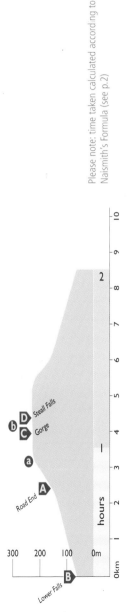

The river drops 400ft (120km) in the gorge; a fall called Eas an Tuill. From the path in the lower gorge there are only glimpses of the river though the roar can be heard clearly. Near the top of the gorge however the path approaches the river and the power of the water can be seen in the smooth rocks, the potholes and cauldrons.

In the 1940s there was a plan to dam the gorge for hydro-electric power. Happily, this came to nothing.

b The path exits abruptly from the gorge into an upland meadow through which the river winds placidly. Easy walking leads beside the river to a notorious and somewhat intimidating bridge consisting of three strands of wire. To cross you walk along the lower wire, using the top two as handrails. The bridge gives access to a white cottage just across the river, a private mountaineering club hut, and also to the foot of Steall Falls. You don't have to cross the bridge to see the falls however. There is a good view just a short distance further on. The path continues up Glen Nevis with good views of the hills to either side so you can walk further if you wish before returning through the gorge.

FORT WILLIAM

Fort William is the major centre for the area and the access point for Glen Nevis. It became known as Fort William after the fort built there in the seventeenth century during the reign of King William III (William of Orange) to control the rebellious Highland clans. No remains of the fort survive.

A curious fact about Fort William is that in 1896 it was the first town in Britain to use hydro-electric power to light its streets.

D Steall Falls 180 682

An Steall Ban – the White Spout – is the third highest waterfall in Scotland and considered by many to be the most impressive. It doesn't lie on the Water of Nevis but on the Allt Coire a'Mhail, a tributary which drains the great corrie that

lies between the peaks of Sgurr a'Mhaim and An Gearanach. An Steall tumbles down the wooded quartzite cliffs that block access to this corrie for 350ft (105m) in a spreading veil of white water, a tremendous sight, especially after heavy rain or during snow melt.

On the path high in the Nevis Gorge

INCHREE WATERFALLS

🖊 🐾 🌱 🍂 🌳

START/FINISH:
Inchree near Corran Ferry on the A82. A small car park and picnic site lies at the end of the short minor road through the hamlet. Gaelicbus from Fort William to Onich 1 mile south along the A82

DISTANCE:
3 miles (5km)

APPROXIMATE TIME:
1½–2 hours

HIGHEST POINT:
525ft (160m)

MAPS:
OS Landranger 41 Ben Nevis, Fort William and surrounding area

REFRESHMENTS:
Café/restaurant on the A82 at Inchree, full facilities in Onich

ADVICE:
An easy walk for a bad weather day

This is a pleasant, easy forest walk on good waymarked paths. It combines two Forestry Commission walks in the Glenrigh Forest, Inchree Waterfall and the Military Road. The waterfalls are particularly spectacular after heavy rain.

A Inchree 025 632

Inchree is a small hamlet just off the A82 road near the Corran Narrows on Loch Linnhe, about 9 miles (15km) from Fort William. The junction is clearly signposted. At the end of the road through the village there is a small car park and picnic site with an information board describing the walks and the forest. The walk starts here.

a From the car park the Inchree Waterfalls path passes through some fields and then across open heather moorland to the narrow cleft of Gleann Righ.

b The path now climbs the hillside above the stream with a good view of one of the falls. A short spur path leads to a viewpoint from which this fall and a larger lower one can be seen clearly. Further on other spurs lead to different views of the falls.

B Inchree Waterfalls 031 629

Also known as the Glen Righ Falls, this series of eight waterfalls on the Abhainn Righ drops some 150ft (45m) down a thickly wooded and narrow ravine. Three of the falls can be seen clearly while others lower down can be heard roaring through the trees. The falls are perhaps at their best after heavy rain in autumn as then the deciduous woodland is a rich mosaic of colour.

c The path leaves the falls and Gleann Righ to climb briefly to a forestry road. Turn left and follow this track as it descends the hillside towards the start point. There are good views down Loch Linnhe to the island of Mull and across the Corran Narrows to the hills of Ardgour. In the distance on a clear day you can apparently see Glensanda quarry, the source of granite chippings for the Channel Tunnel, though I can't say I've ever picked it out. I'd rather look at the hills, woods and loch anyway.

Inchree Waterfalls

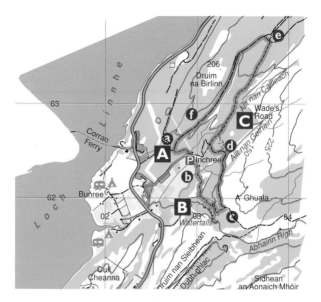

d   The track enters the forest and comes to a junction where a path marked 'forest walk' heads off to the right (north-east).

C   Wade's Road   038 648

Wade's Road is an old military road built in the 1750s, which originally went all the way to Fort William. The name suggests it was built by General George Wade who was appointed commander in Scotland after the collapse of the 1715 Jacobite rising and who built the first roads in the Highlands between 1724 and 1736. However this road postdates Wade and was built by General Caulfield, one of his successors.

e   The path climbs quite steeply through the spruce and larch plantations with some views of the surrounding hills until, after a mile (1.6km) or so, it reaches another forestry road beside a small disused quarry marked Wade's Road. The forest stretches much further to the north-east along the side of Loch Linnhe but to return to the start turn left (south-west) and descend the track. If you want a longer walk you can continue along the road for just over a mile (1.6km) to another Forestry Commission waymarked walk at Corrychurrachan which leads down to a car park on the A82.

f   Just above Inchree a sign marks the point where a path leaves the track and descends into the hamlet. A short waymarked path leads back to the start.

Inchree Waterfalls

Please note: time taken calculated according to Naismith's Formula (see p.2)

MAMORE LODGE

START/FINISH:
Kinlochleven. There is a
Gaelicbus from Fort William

DISTANCE:
4 miles (6.5km)

APPROXIMATE TIME:
2–3 hours

HIGHEST POINT:
900ft (270m)

MAPS:
Harvey's Walker's Map &
Superwalker Ben Nevis, OS
Outdoor Leisure 38 Ben Nevis
& Glen Coe, OS Landranger 41
Ben Nevis, Fort William and
surrounding area

REFRESHMENTS:
Snacks and drinks at Mamore
Lodge, halfway through the
walk. All facilities in
Kinlochleven

ADVICE:
Although only short some of
this walk is on steep rough
paths that can be slippery
when wet so hill walking
footwear is essential

There is much to see on this short walk, which takes you past a dramatic waterfall then climbs steeply to a track that runs across the hillside past Mamore Lodge, where refreshments are available, before descending along part of the West Highland Way long distance path. There are superb views down Loch Leven and of the surrounding hills as well as birch woodlands that are particularly colourful in the autumn.

A Kinlochleven 187 619
Kinlochleven lies at the head of beautiful Loch Leven, a long narrow fjord-like sea loch, and is hemmed in by mountains. Although the main industry is the aluminium smelter (see Walk 8 for more information on this) the small town is well-provided with facilities for walkers as the popular West Highland Way long distance path passes through the town, bringing tens of thousands of walkers every year. The useful Visitor Centre houses an interesting display on the aluminium industry.

a Opposite the police station on the B863 road through Kinlochmore, the part of Kinlochleven that lies north of the River Leven, a signpost for the Grey Mare's Waterfall points down Kieran Road towards a white church. There is a small car park beside the church from which a waymarked path heads up the wooded hillside. The walk begins here.

b The well-made path climbs through a mixture of birch trees and bracken. The path divides soon after the start, keep left here. (The right fork heads up to Loch Eilde Mor and the Eastern Mamores as described in Walk 22). The falls can be heard before they are first seen through a screen of trees. The path descends slightly into a shady wooded glen and crosses a small burn on a wooden footbridge. There is another fork here. For a close up look at the falls take the left fork, which leads through the trees to the burn just beyond the foot of the falls, a superb viewpoint.

B The Grey Mare's Fall 187 625
This is one of the most impressive waterfalls in the area, indeed in all of Scotland according to some. The setting is beautiful and spectacular. The Allt Coire na Ba tumbles 150ft

The Grey Mare's Fall

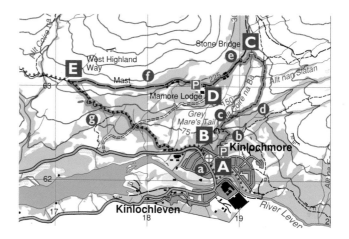

(46m) over a sheer cliff rimmed with pine trees into a narrow, steep-sided, wooded gorge. From the path end the main plunge of the falls is seen but both the bottom and top are hidden from view. If the burn isn't too full of water it's possible, with care as the spray-soaked mossy rocks are slippery, to reach the pool at the foot of the falls. In spring the woodland floor is covered with bluebells.

c After viewing the falls retrace your steps to the footbridge and, without crossing it, continue up the steep path ahead. There are a couple of side paths that lead off from the main one towards the top of the falls. These give views down the falls and also of some smaller falls that lie above the main one. However the viewpoints are right on the edge of the gorge in somewhat precarious situations and the paths are often slippery and muddy so great care is needed.

d The rough, stony path zigzags steeply northwards up a spur between two stream gorges. The climb eases as the last birch trees are left behind and the path starts to curve left into the glen of the Allt Coire na Ba. There are splendid views down the length of Loch Leven with the pointed peaks of Beinn na Caillich and the Pap of Glencoe (see Walks 9 & 12) soaring above the dark waters. A couple of small burns are forded then the path splits. Avoid the first path to the left which crosses the Allt Coire na Ba lower down, the branch we want heads north-westwards and curves down to an old arched bridge over the Allt Coire na Ba.

C The Stone Bridge 192 634

This humpback bridge is very attractive and in a wonderful situation with the peaks of the Mamores rising above it to the north and rich woodlands running down to Loch Leven to the south. The bridge is deteriorating. At its narrowest it is only 3ft (1m) wide; cross with care.

e Beyond the bridge the path climbs briefly to join a wide track at a large open area. Turn left on this track and follow it to a white house and some smaller buildings. A signposted path leads round the front of the house to a track on the far side of the cluster of buildings. Not far along this track another, larger building appears below the track. This is Mamore Lodge.

Climbing through the trees above Kinlochleven

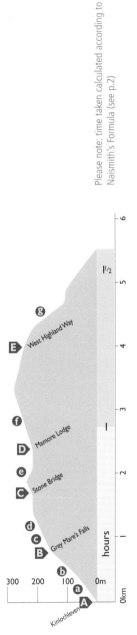

Please note: time taken calculated according to Naismith's Formula (see p.2)

D Mamore Lodge 186 629

Set high on the steep hillside above Loch Leven Mamore Lodge is wonderfully situated. Originally a private lodge, with King Edward VII as its most famous guest in 1909, it now belongs to Alcan, the aluminium smelting company, along with the rest of the estate, and is run as a hotel. It's a good base for exploring the Mamores. It's also open for refreshments and so a good place for a rest, especially in inclement weather. The garden round the Lodge contains cedars, rhododendrons and other trees and shrubs that are unusual in this setting.

f   The track continues across the hillside past the Lodge with magnificent views of the hills either side of Loch Leven. After passing a television mast a junction is reached with the

The stone bridge over the Allt Coire Ba

West Highland Way which here follows the line of General Caulfield's military road to Fort William, built in the mid-1700s. Our route turns sharply left here (south-east) and descends steeply through birch woods back to Kinlochleven, crossing on the way the tarmac road leading to Mamore Lodge.

E   West Highland Way 172 631

The West Highland Way is an official well-waymarked long distance path under the auspices of Scottish Natural Heritage. It runs for 92 miles (148km) from Milngavie, not far north of Glasgow, to Fort William, passing through rather than over the hills on paths, forestry tracks, and old roads. It's very popular and tens of thousands of walkers complete it every year. The West Highland Way enters the area of this

guidebook at the head of Glen Etive, after coming round the east side of the Blackmount Hills on the edge of Rannoch Moor, then crosses the Devil's Staircase to Kinlochleven and then over another pass to Fort William.

g The West Highland Way reaches the B863 opposite the school. To return to the centre of Kinlochleven simply follow the road. To return to the Grey Mare's Falls car park take the first left turn and follow this road as it curves round to the car park.

View down to Loch Leven with Sgurr na Ciche on the left and Beinn na Caillich on the right

GLENCOE FOREST WALKS

Pleasant mixed woodlands cover the little knoll of Torr a Chomhain and the lower slopes of the Pap of Glencoe at the foot of Glen Coe. A small lochan lies at the heart of this forest. The Forestry Commission has laid out three easy walks here, all of them pleasant strolls with views of the surrounding hills. Rhododendrons give a splash of colour in spring and there are many fine trees.

START/FINISH:
Glencoe village. Gaelicbus from Fort William

DISTANCE:
Max 4 miles (6.5km)

APPROXIMATE TIME:
2–3 hours

HIGHEST POINT: 345ft (105m)

MAPS:
Harvey's Walker's Map & Superwalker Glen Coe, OS Outdoor Leisure 38 Ben Nevis & Glen Coe, OS Landranger 41 Ben Nevis, Fort William and surrounding area

REFRESHMENTS:
Glencoe village

ADVICE:
A good evening stroll. Could be combined with Walks 3 or 4 on a day when the clouds are down on the hills. The Lochan Walk has wheelchair access

A Glencoe village 098 587

Glencoe village consists mainly of one street, the old road through the glen, at the head of which soars Sgorr na Ciche (the Pap of Glencoe – see Walk 12). There is a Folk Museum in the village in an old black thatched, white-washed, low-ceilinged cottage, which is worth a visit.

Beside the Hospital Lochan with Sgurr na Ciche in the background

a To get to the start of the walks drive or walk down the main street and cross the old mossy humpbacked bridge over the River Coe. There is a Celtic cross here, erected 'in memory of MacIan, Chief of Glen Coe, who fell with his people in the Massacre of Glencoe'. Just beyond the bridge the road bends right and there is a side road signposted for the Hospital. Take this road to where it divides, then follow the right fork up to a car park where there is an information board.

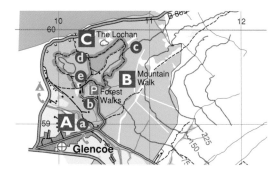

b Three walks are laid out in the forest. These can be combined to give a round trip. Start with the Mountain Walk, a gravel path that begins in the upper right corner of the car park. Climbing fairly steeply through a dense rhododendron

View over the Hospital Lochan to Beinn Caillich

'jungle' and some Scots pine the path gives good views, especially west to Beinn a'Bheithir (see Walk 23). There are several benches during the ascent. Near the top of the climb there is a first view of the lochan to the north.

B   Mountain Walk Viewpoint 106 596

At the high point of the walk there is a picnic table and seat. The views are extensive, particularly to the west where, as well as the long ridges and pointed peaks of Beinn a'Bheithir, you can look down the long narrow length of Loch Leven over tiny-looking Ballachulish Bridge to Loch Linnhe and, beyond it, the rugged mountain of Garbh Bheinn, some 10 miles (6km) away. Only to the east do trees block the view though Sgorr na Ciche (the Pap of Glencoe) can be seen a little further down the path.

Please note: time taken calculated according to Naismith's Formula (see p.2)

c The path descends steeply to the east end of the lochan and a wide track. This is the Lochan Trail. You can go either way here but I suggest going round the northern side of the lochan.

C The Lochan 107 598

The lochan is artificial and was built by Lord Strathcona in the late-nineteenth century. He also laid out the surrounding estate and built Glencoe House, which is now Glencoe Hospital, hence the name 'Hospital Lochan' that is often used. As David Alexander Smith Lord Strathcona had emigrated to Canada where he became first Governor of the Hudson's Bay Company and then High Commissioner to Canada. He also married a half-native Canadian woman and it was for her that he created the estate in the hope that this corner of the Highlands could be made to resemble her Canadian home enough to overcome her homesickness. Unsurprisingly this did not work and they returned to live in Canada. The estate is now owned by the Forestry Commission. There are

The Hospital Lochan at dusk

wonderful views over the lochan to the surrounding hills, especially when the water is calm and full of reflections. There are a few wooded islets in the lochan.

d   At the north-west end of the lochan a track leading off to the right away from the lochan forms the Woodland Walk. This path makes a circuit through some of the old estate woodlands with short side paths that lead to picnic tables and seats at viewpoints over Loch Leven. The planted forest includes some fine Douglas Fir and Sequoias along with a mix of deciduous trees. The path after passing a lily pond returns to the car park. Alternatively, keep to the side of the lochan following a metal railing across the earth dam that holds in the waters of the lochan.

e   Where the path divides take the left fork and pass under an arch of rowan trees to a small lily pond. There's another fork at the arch. The left fork will take you back to the lochan and a small wooden hut, the right one to the car park.

THE MASSACRE OF GLENCOE

Glencoe is best known outside hillwalking and mountaineering circles for the infamous massacre. This occurred in 1692 against a background of the 1688 rising against the King, William of Orange, and years of raids on each other's territories by the Highland clans. The government offered a pardon in August 1691 to those involved in the 1688 rising. To gain this pardon, the alternative to which was death, the clan chief had to take an oath of allegiance before a magistrate by January 1, 1692. The Chief of the MacDonalds of Glen Coe, Maclain, put off swearing the oath for as long as possible, probably both because he was an old man and did not relish a long journey in winter and because he hated the idea of swearing allegiance to the crown. Finally Maclain rode to Inverlochy (later renamed as Fort William) where he was told he had to go on to Inverary. He arrived two days later to find the sheriff away and so had to wait another three days before he could swear the oath, on January 6, five days late.

Maclain returned to Glen Coe, feeling he was now safe. However at the end of January a party of troops arrived in the glen, headed by Captain Robert Campbell of Glen Lyon. He had no reason to be friendly to the MacDonalds as they had raided Glen Lyon and stolen all the cattle there. Campbell asked for lodging for his soldiers, giving his word that they would do no harm, and the MacDonalds took them in. For ten days all was well but then Campbell received orders from Major Robert Duncanson at Inverlochy telling him 'to put all to sword under seventy'. The massacre began the next morning, in a blizzard. Some 38 people were slaughtered, including Maclain and his wife, but hundreds more escaped into the hills, many to die of cold and hunger. Most however survived and returned to live in the glen.

Why has the massacre, which after all was just one in a whole series of bloody and violent events, carried such resonance down the years? The general view is that it's because of the betrayal of hospitality, the treachery of turning on ones hosts, that the event has been remembered.

A video presentation on the massacre plus much other information on Glen Coe can be found in the National Trust for Scotland Visitor Centre, which is situated in the glen near the site of the massacre but which is to be moved to the NTS camp site further down the glen.

AN TORR AND SIGNAL ROCK

This walk could be combined with a visit to these rock outcrops, a half hour walk from the NTS Visitor Centre. They are situated in pleasant woods. An Torr gives good views up Glen Coe and up Gleann-Leac-na-Muidhe to the south. Signal Rock is said to be the place where a fire was lit early in the morning of February 13, 1692, as a sign that the massacre should start.

GLEN ETIVE & THE ROBBER'S WATERFALL

Glen Etive is a magnificent glen with a remote wild feel to it. A narrow single-track road runs down the glen, giving access to many hills. This walk follows the banks of the lower River Etive before climbing slightly to a fine waterfall on a tributary stream. As well as the falls there are cascades, deep pools, small cliffs and fringes of trees, all backed by high mountains.

A   Glen Etive

Lying so close to Glen Coe it's surprising how empty Glen Etive can be. There are no facilities in the glen however and the 12-mile (20-kilometre) single-track road that twists and turns down the glen is a cul-de-sac, dead-ending at the end of

START/FINISH:
Lower Glen Etive GR 136 467.
Postbus (Monday to Saturday)
to Glen Etive Post Office from
Fort William and Glencoe

DISTANCE: 5 miles
(8km)

APPROXIMATE TIME:
2–3 hours

HIGHEST POINT:
688ft (210m)

MAPS:
Harvey's Walker's Map &
Superwalker Glen Coe, OS
Landranger 50 Glen Orchy and
surrounding area

REFRESHMENTS:
None in Glen Etive. The
Kingshouse Hotel just beyond
the head of Glen Etive is the
nearest place for refreshments

ADVICE:
A pleasant riverside stroll for a
lazy evening or a day off from
longer hill walks. The walk up
to the Robber's Waterfall is
steep and can be muddy and
slippery after rain

The River Etive

The River Etive and Stob Dubh

Loch Etive. There's no reason to go down the glen then except for the scenery, the mountains and woods, the river and loch, the plants and wildlife. The glen offers many opportunities for high level walks in the hills (see Walks 15, 16, 26, 27 & 28) and it's also visited by canoeists, who run the small rapids on the river, and rock climbers heading for the Trilleachan Slabs (see Walk 7). To reach Glen Etive turn off the A82 at the signposted junction opposite the road that leads to the Kingshouse Hotel.

The upper glen on the north-west side of the River Etive above the house at Dalness is owned by the National Trust for Scotland. The terrain here is open moorland, quickly rising to

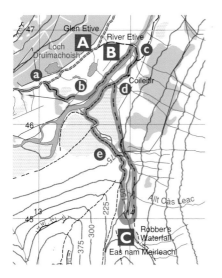

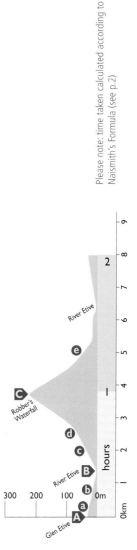

Please note: time taken calculated according to Naismith's Formula (see p.2)

the rugged, rocky heights of the Buachaille Etive Mor (see Walk 25) and Creise (see Walk 26). Like other glens it was wooded once and there are a few remnants of the old Caledonian forest, clinging to little crags and steep slopes above the river where they are out of reach of the destructive browsing of sheep and deer. A narrow section between the road and river about a mile (1.6km) long has been fenced off to keep out grazing animals and allow the regeneration of the pine forest. This is called the Allt Chaorunn Caledonian Forest.

Below Dalness the right (north-west) side of the glen has been heavily planted with spruce and larch, but over the river the terrain is still mostly boggy moorland with a few remnants of the old Caledonian forest in places.

a There are a number of small parking places beside the road in the lower glen. The walk itself starts where a track leaves the road (GR 131 464) and runs down to the river.

b At the river bank turn left and follow a path above the rushing waters. Ahead is a narrow section where the river runs through a small gorge with rocky wooded walls. A large footbridge crosses the river here, with views down into the dark pools below. Although perched high above the river this bridge is below the high water mark of the river which occurred in 1906 when a flash flood raised the level 23 ft (7m) or more.

In Celtic legend Glen Etive is the land of Deirdre of the Sorrows. She was a beautiful Irish woman who took shelter in Glen Etive with her lover Naisi or Naoise in order to evade King Conor of Ulster. However Conor sent his son Fergus to bring them back and they returned to their deaths. As they sailed away down Glen Etive Deirdre sang a lament in which she remembered the beauty of the glen and how happy she had been.

B   River Etive 140 468

The River Etive is a delightful stream. There are no dramatic waterfalls but it tumbles over many little rock steps, trickles over wide pebble beds and boulders and slows down in deep, dark, peaty brown pools. The banks in the lower glen are lined with alders, birches, holly, rowan and the occasional Scots pine. It is particularly attractive in autumn when the leaves of the deciduous trees turn red and gold, while in spring flowers decorate the banks. Although there are bigger hills close by the steep splendid cone of 2,896ft- (883m-) Stob Dubh dominates the view.

c   Just across the bridge there are two choices as the track soon divides. Up the glen it follows the river for ½ mile (800m) or so to Glenceitlein where it peters out though you could continue further before retracing your steps unless the river is low enough to be forded and the road followed back to the start.

d   Turning right at the fork you quickly reach the house at Coileitir where the track becomes a path which then soon divides. Take the left fork that climbs across some boggy ground through open birch woodland to the Allt Mheuran. A fenced area here ensures the future of the trees by keeping out deer though, as elsewhere, a reduction in deer numbers would be a better solution than preserving isolated patches of forest. Then large areas could return to natural woodland. The Robber's Waterfall lies about ⅔ mile (1km) up the Allt Mheuran.

C   Eas nam Meirleach (The Robber's Waterfall) 139 450

The Eas nam Meirleach is oddly named as it lies on the Allt Mheuran rather than the Allt Meirleach which is just to the west and which joins the Mheuran below the falls. It's called the Robber's Waterfall either because stolen cattle were concealed in the ravine at its foot, or according to Louis Stott in his *Waterfalls of Scotland*, because cattle thieves rested here. The main fall is a 50ft- (15m-) freefall double drop into a dark, narrow, twisted tree-rimmed gorge. Above this a series of cascades tumbles down a tributary stream. The situation is magnificent with views across Glen Etive to massive Bidean nam Bian (see Walk 24). The best place to see the waterfall is from below. Higher up you have to approach the edge rather too closely for comfort to gain much of a view. There are some attractive waterslides a little higher up the stream that are worth a look if you want to go on further.

E Below the falls the Allt Mheuran can be forded without difficulty except after heavy rain. In late summer high bracken, which is often home to ticks, can impede progress. A path on the far bank leads down to a footbridge back across the stream and a path that leads back to Coileitir, the bridge over the River Etive and the start.

The Robber's Waterfall

LOCH ETIVE SHORE WALK & THE TRILLEACHAN SLABS

START/FINISH:
Lower Glen Etive. Postbus (Monday to Saturday) to Glen Etive Post Office from Fort William and Glencoe

DISTANCE:
3 miles (5km) to Aird Trilleachan

APPROXIMATE TIME:
2–3 hours

HIGHEST POINT:
1,000ft (305m)

MAPS:
OS Landranger 50 Glen Orchy and the surrounding area

REFRESHMENTS:
None in Glen Etive. The Kingshouse Hotel just beyond the head of Glen Etive is the nearest place serving food and drink

ADVICE:
Although short this walk is on muddy footpaths and steep hillsides in a remote area so appropriate footwear and clothing is needed

Rocky slopes rise either side of narrow Loch Etive covered with a scattering of old forest. This walk climbs to the base of some steep and spectacular granite slabs, from where there are superb views of Glen Etive, then descends to return along the loch shore. The walking is on steep and muddy terrain giving the walk a seriousness belied by the short distance.

A   Loch Etive   108 450

Loch Etive is a magnificent fjord-like sea loch. Unusually there are no roads on either side of the long narrow upper arm, which stretches 10 miles (15km), into the hills from the narrows between Taynuilt and Bonawe. (There are motor cruises up the loch from Taynuilt in summer.) This makes it a superb area for walkers. Steep, rugged hills rise above the loch. From their slopes there are superb views of Glen Etive. Paths run down both sides of the loch.

Loch Etive

Loch Etive and Glen Etive from the base of the Trilleachan Slabs

a At the road end there is a decaying old pier and a few dilapidated buildings plus room for a few cars. The path to the Trilleachan Slabs starts just beyond the road, heading south-west up the steep, rough lower slopes of 2,752ft (839m) Beinn Trilleachan.

b The path is rough and can be muddy after rain but there are no difficulties until you reach about 610ft (the 200m contour on the map) after a ¼ mile (400m) or so. Here there are a couple of awkward rock steps that are slippery when wet, but these can be avoided by steep diversions across the tussocky ground surrounding them.

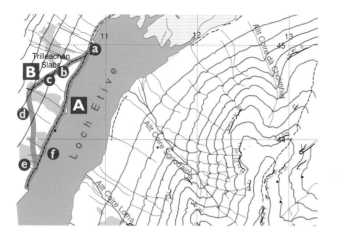

c After 1,000ft (300m) of climbing the base of the Trilleachan Slabs is reached.

B The Trilleachan Slabs 102 446

These huge and impressive slabs, also known as the Etive Slabs, are a famous rock-climbing venue and you may well see climbers balancing precariously on the sloping rock. The angle is such that they can be climbed by friction alone rather than by using definite holds. None of the climbs are easy though and there are no routes up the slabs for scramblers. If you want to continue up Beinn Trilleachan there is a way up a gully just beyond the slabs that leads to the ridge ½ mile (0.8km) or so before the summit. Alternatively you can take the route described in Walk 16. At the base of the slabs is a large flat rock called the Coffin Stone, often used by climbers for sorting out their gear. From here there are superb views down to Loch Etive and back up the glen.

d There is no path down to the loch from the base of the slabs but a route can easily be found by angling down southwards towards a small birch wood. The ground inside the wood is very rough with many boulders so it's best to keep to the edge of it. Further down there are more small woods, of birch at first then mainly of oak as the loch is approached. On the descent there is a 2m (6ft) deer fence near the loch. To find the stile follow the deer fence back towards the loch.

e Once the path along the loch shore is reached you can either return to the road end or continue for some way along the loch. I'd suggest continuing at least to the point of Aird Trilleachan, further if you have the time. There are more

Please note: time taken calculated according to Naismith's Formula (see p.2)

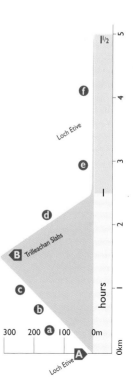

The Trilleachan Slabs

woods, mostly oak though with holly, rowan hazel and alder
as well – the remains of the old Caledonian Forest that once
blanketed Glen Etive. Some of the old trees are quite
magnificent, a reminder of lost glories. A mile (1.6km) or so
beyond Aird Trilleachan however the woods become thicker
and change to dense plantations so I wouldn't go further than
this. The shore path is rough in places and there are many
easy fords as it crosses the myriad streams that pour down
from the slopes of Beinn Trilleachan. Across the loch rise the
steep, forbidding slopes of 3,541ft (1,078m) Ben Starav, riven
by deep gullies (see Walk 28) while down the loch rise the
twin peaks of 3,695ft (1,126m) Ben Cruachan, one of the
finest mountains in the Southern Highlands.

f   The route back along the loch shore is very wet, especially
on the last section below the Trilleachan Slabs. The views up
the glen make up for the dampness underfoot however.

THE BLACKWATER RESERVOIR

This unusual walk mixes scenic beauty with industrial history. The story of the aluminium works and the building of the reservoir is an interesting one whatever one thinks of such developments. The walk takes the form of a circuit of the attractive wooded glen of the River Leven.

A   Kinlochleven & The Visitor Centre

Kinlochleven is a small industrial town dominated by the aluminium works, the reason for its existence. Indeed, it was almost called Aluminiumville. Before the works opened in 1904 there were just two tiny hamlets here, Kinlochbeg south of the River Leven and Kinlochmore to the north. These merged to become Kinlochleven though maps often still name Kinlochmore. The Visitor Centre, itself made of aluminium, houses an interesting display on the aluminium industry which I recommend seeing before doing this walk as it explains much that is seen along the way.

a   From the Visitor Centre follow the main road (B863) across the bridge over the River Leven. Immediately over the bridge a West Highland Way sign points the way along the side of the River Leven with a good view of the tremendous surge of water of the power station outflow. This initial path comes out on Wades Road where you turn right and follow the road to the end of the houses where it becomes a track. The West

START/FINISH:
Kinlochleven; car park adjacent to visitor's centre. There is a Gaelicbus from Fort William

DISTANCE:
12 miles (19km)

APPROXIMATE TIME: 6 hours

HIGHEST POINT:
1,080ft (330m)

MAPS:
Harvey's Walker's Map & Superwalker Glen Coe, OS Outdoor Leisure 38 Ben Nevis & Glen Coe, OS Landranger 41 Ben Nevis, Fort William, Fort William and surrounding area

REFRESHMENTS:
Kinlochleven has cafes, chip shops and bars

ADVICE:
Although it doesn't venture high in the hills this is a long walk into remote country so full day walking gear should be carried. Heavy rain may cause many burns to become impassable

Start of the path to the Blackwater Reservoir

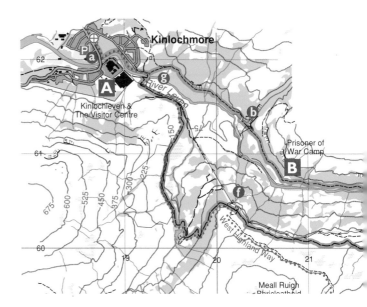

Highland Way crosses a bridge over the river here. At the 'Ciaran Path' signpost the main track branches three ways. Take the central (less distinct) path going uphill. The terrain is wooded here, mostly with birch, but there are also some splendid large oaks as well as beech, larch and Scots pine. In

The Blackwater Reservoir

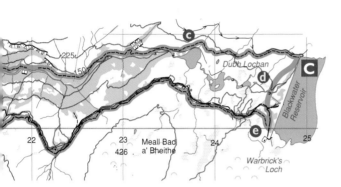

summer the surrounding vegetation is quite lush and the path can be quite overgrown.

b   The path (or paths as there are several variations) winds through the woods beside the river to a small wooded gorge where it crosses a bridge over the Allt na h-Eilde which drains Loch Eilde Mor high above on the slopes of the Mamores (see Walk 21). There is a nice waterfall just to the left here. Soon after the bridge there is a flat area with the concrete bases of buildings spread everywhere. This is an old P.O.W. camp.

B   The Prisoner of War Camp   207 607
The ragged patches of concrete are the remains of a First World War P.O.W. camp which held over 1,000 German prisoners. These captives built the pipeline that runs from Loch Eilde Mor to the Blackwater Reservoir and also the road from Kinlochleven to Glencoe.

c   Beyond the camp the path continues along the side of the wooded glen with occasional views down to the River Leven, which in places runs through some impressive rocky gorges. There is a bridge over an unnamed burn at GR 232 608 which is in a dangerous condition. This can be bypassed nearby upstream. Just over a mile (1.6km) from the reservoir the path climbs out of the enclosed glen onto open moorland by the two pools known as the Dubh Lochan. The huge dam can be seen blocking the glen ahead. For the final stretch to the dam the path runs close to the pipeline bringing water from Loch Eilde Mor.

C   The Blackwater Reservoir 249 608

From the edge of the dam the bleak waters of the Blackwater Reservoir can be seen stretching away into the distance. The hills on either side are low and don't rise much above the water and the feeling is one of vastness and space. The reservoir is 8 miles (13km) long, drowning the glen of the Black Water which once held three lochans. It also flooded part of the old drove road from Loch Treig to Kingshouse. The best view from the dam is south to the great soaring bulk of the Buachaille Etive Mor (see Walk 25).

Like most of the reservoirs that fill all too many glens in the Highlands the Blackwater was built to provide hydroelectric power rather than drinking water. This however was one of the very earliest hydro schemes, most of them were built after the Second World War. Huge amounts of electricity are needed for aluminium smelting which is why the industry was sited in Kinlochleven where advantage could be taken of water power to provide that electricity. One spin-off was that Kinlochleven was one of the first towns in Britain to have electric street lighting. The dam was built between 1904–09 by thousands of navvies who camped on the exposed and desolate moorland nearby. Many died in the harsh weather, often when returning from forays to the distant Kingshouse Hotel. Some are buried in a small graveyard near the dam on the south side of the river. The walk goes past this. The story of the dam is told in fictional form in the novel *Children of the Dead End*, whose author, Patrick McGill, was one of the navvies. The dam is over ½ mile long (800m) with an average height of 80ft (24m) and a width at the base of over 60ft (18m). And it was all built with pick and shovel.

d   The walkway across the dam is closed to the public and the gate padlocked but a way can be made below it, though this involves a little route finding as there's no path and the ground is broken and dotted with shrubs and small trees. Near the far side of the dam is the concrete slab covered conduit that carries the water along the side of the glen to the penstock from where six massive pipes take it steeply down to the power station. The water roars out of the base of the dam and into the conduit in great surges.

e Beside the conduit a track runs along the side of the glen back towards Kinlochleven. This gives easy walking with superb views north to the long line of the Mamores and down to the River Leven.

The outflow from the Blackwater dam

f A couple of miles from Kinlochleven the West Highland Way joins the track, having come over from the south by the pass known as the Devil's Staircase. This is the route of General Caulfield's military road, built in 1749–50. The track starts to descend now, curving round the bowl of the Allt Coire Mhorair. To the right six enormous pipelines plunge steeply straight down the hillside, building up a huge head of water.

g Once down in the glen the path reaches the footbridge over the river that was passed earlier. From there our outwards route leads back into Kinlochleven.

MAM NA GUALAINN & BEINN NA CAILLICH

START/FINISH:
Kinlochleven. There is a Gaelicbus from Fort William and Citylink buses also go via Kinlochleven

DISTANCE:
11 miles (18km)

APPROXIMATE TIME:
6–9 hours

HIGHEST POINT:
2,610ft (796m) Mam na Gualainn

MAPS:
Harvey's Walker's Map & Superwalker Ben Nevis, OS Outdoor Leisure 38 Ben Nevis & Glen Coe, OS Landranger 41 Ben Nevis, Fort William and surrounding area

REFRESHMENTS:
Kinlochleven has cafes, chip shops and bars. Mamore Lodge also serves refreshments

ADVICE:
The only difficulties could be in route finding between the two summits, as there are only bits of path. The ground is very boggy in places. A compass should be used if visibility is bad

These two hills, south-western outliers of the Mamores, give superb views of Loch Leven and its surroundings. The ascent, mostly on a good stalking path, is easy but long.

a   The walk starts in Kinlochleven. From the Visitor Centre follow the main road through the town (the B863) across the bridge over the River Leven, then the smaller Corrie Bridge over the Allt Coire na Ba. Not far beyond the last bridge the school is reached on the left. Across the road a signpost and information board indicate where the West Highland Way begins its final section to Fort William. It's also where this walk starts.

b Follow the West Highland Way, here a stony path, as it climbs steeply through graceful birch woods with good views back down to Loch Leven. After ¼ mile (400m) the tarmac road to Mamore Lodge is crossed. (Mamore Lodge is an alternative start point, with the advantage of being 650ft (200m) higher than Kinlochleven. For a fee you can leave your car in the Lodge car park for the day. If you do start here turn left along the track from the Lodge and follow it to where it joins the West Highland Way. (See Walk 4 for more information.)

c The path leaves the trees and soon afterwards joins the track from Mamore Lodge where it crosses a small spur called the Mam Mor or Big Pass. Climbing more gently now the path crosses the Allt Coire na h-Eirghe and curves westward into the empty glen of the Allt Nathrach, which can be seen down to the left. This is the line of General Caulfield's military road, built in 1749–50, which continues to Fort William. The huge

Loch Leven and the lower slopes of Mam na Gualainn

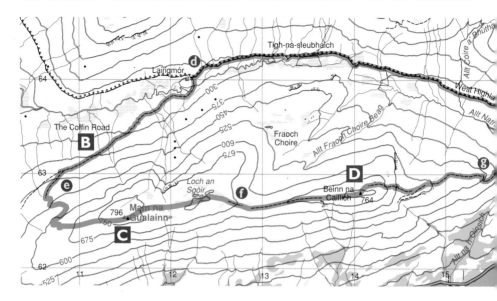

rugged hill ahead and to the right is 3,274ft (999 m) Stob Ban in the Mamores. The pale summit is made from quartzite, a hard, angular rock that can look white in some lights.

A   Loch Leven and Beinn na Caillich
Before entering the enclosed Allt Nathrach glen there is a superb view of Loch Leven and the hills rising beyond it. Ahead the very steep eastern end of Beinn na Caillich dominates the view. A footpath can be seen climbing the nose in tight zigzags. This is our descent route.

d   The track continues up to a boggy watershed, the Lairig Mor or Big Pass, at the head of the Allt Nathrach at 1,000ft (305m) and passes the ruined house of Tigh-na-sleubhaich, once a stalker's dwelling, then starts to descend into the glen of the Allt na Lairige Moire. After another mile (1.6km) or so another ruined house, Lairigmor, is reached. Here we leave the track for a path that heads south-west. Crossing the burn after Lairigmor could be difficult after heavy rain. The steep stony northern slopes of Mam na Gualainn dominate the view.

B   The Coffin Road   122 640
The path from Lairigmor runs for 3 miles (5km) over the shoulder of Mam na Gualainn to Callert on Loch Leven. This is an old coffin road along which the dead were carried to be ferried from Callert out to the island of Eilean Munde (the Island of the World) to be buried, safe from predation by

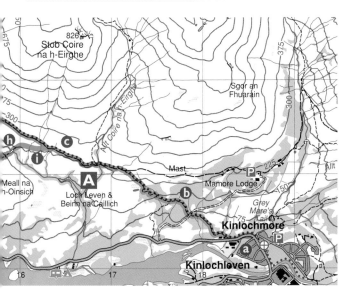

wolves. This island and the surrounding islets can be seen from the summit of Mam na Gualainn on a clear day. The island is named after St Fintan Mundus, an Irish disciple of St Columba of Iona fame, who built a church on it around 600 AD. The landing places on Eilean Munde were called the Ports of the Dead and each of the clans who used the island as a burial ground – the MacDonalds of Glencoe, Camerons of Callert and Stewarts of Ballachulish – had their own port. Apparently, the MacDonalds killed in the Massacre of Glencoe (see Walk 5) were buried on Eilean Munde. Burials continued on the island into the 1950s.

e   A bit over a mile (1.6km) from Lairigmor, not far before the high point on the Callert path, a smaller path forks off to the left. Take this old stalker's path, which climbs to a height of 1,700ft (518m) on the western slopes of Mam na Gualainn. From here it is an easy walk up the broad west ridge to the summit. In mist head on a magnetic bearing of 125 to gain the ridge and then a bearing of magnetic 60 to reach the summit.

C   Mam na Gualainn 115 625
From the summit of Mam na Gualainn there are extensive views all around except to the east, where Beinn na Caillich blocks more distant hills. Especially dramatic is Beinn a'Bheithir (see Walk 23) whose long ridges rise from Loch Leven to the pointed summits.

Please note: time taken calculated according to Naismith's Formula (see p.2)

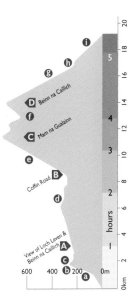

Beinn na Caillich

Mam means a rounded hill, from the Gaelic word for breast, while Gualainn means shoulder, so Mam na Gualainn is the Hill of the Shoulder according to Peter Drummond (*Scottish Hill and Mountain Names*). Drummond explains this by saying that the name describes the shape of the hill and its position as an outlier, or shoulder, of the Mamores. However other people give the name as the Pass of the Shoulder as 'mam' can also mean a pass, that is the dip between two breasts. In that case perhaps the name has been transferred from the low pass on the western shoulder of the hill crossed by the path to Callert.

Whatever the meaning of the name, Mam na Gualainn is classified as a Corbett, that is a hill between 2,500ft (762m) and 3,000ft (914.4m) with a drop of at least 500ft (152.4m) between it and the next hill. There are 220 Corbetts in total. They are listed in Munro's Tables.

f From Mam na Gualainn it's just over a mile (1.6km) of high level walking to the subsidiary summit of Beinn na Caillich. There is no path for much of the way and a compass will be needed unless it's clear. After an initial short descent the route crosses a minor top then descends to the small col between the peaks at 2,165ft (660m). The broad slopes of Mam na Gualainn are behind us now and the west ridge of Beinn na

Caillich is narrow though without difficulties. There is a clear path from the col to the second summit.

D   Beinn na Caillich 141 628

Although the lower of the two hills, Beinn na Caillich is by far the finer in appearance. Where Mam na Gualainn, as the name suggests, is a rounded lump, Beinn na Caillich is a more graceful, pointed peak. It looks especially impressive from the slopes above Kinlochleven (see Walk 4) but also stands out in views across Loch Leven to the south.

The views from the peak are also good. There are two cairns. From one the long dark line of the Blackwater Reservoir can be seen, from the other Loch Leven, the houses of Ballachulish and Glencoe and the hills beyond them. Also in sight is the artificial lochan in the forest above Glencoe village (see Walk 5). To the north the Mamores dominate the scene.

g   When preparing for your descent from the second summit, locate the eastern of the two cairns and from there head due north for about 650ft (200m). You have to negotiate small gullies and bluffs at the same time as descending steeply for about 300ft (90m) and then you arrive in a small dip or hollow from which there is a well-defined zigzag path heading east which leads under the low crags and rocks that lie east of the summit. This then leads down the hillside to the Allt Nathrach.

h   There is a bridge over the Allt Nathrach, but if it is unusuable then it may be advisable to ford the stream. Immediately below the bridge the stream runs through a small, steep-sided, rocky gorge so a crossing cannot be made here. There are possibilities both above and below the bridge. On my last visit I crossed about 100 yards (91m) below the bridge, stepping from boulder to boulder to keep my boots dry. When the stream is in spate crossing could be difficult. In that case it might be better to do this walk the other way round so the ford can be tackled early in the day and an easy retreat made if it proves impossible. Alternatively, a descent from Beinn na Caillich could be made by returning to the col with Mam na Gualainn and descending north-east into the corrie to the Allt Fraoch Choire Beag. This stream can be followed down into the upper Allt Nathrach glen where the boggy ground and small streams can be easily crossed to the West Highland Way.

i   Once across the Allt Nathrach a boggy path leads up to the West Highland Way which can then be followed back to Kinlochleven.

GARBH BHEINN

START/FINISH:
Caolasnacon, Loch Leven.
There is a Gaelicbus from Fort
William. Small parking spaces
can be found beside the B863
near the bridge over the Allt
Gleann a'Chaolais (GR 145
608)

DISTANCE:
4 miles (6km)

APPROXIMATE TIME:
4–6 hours

HIGHEST POINT:
2,845ft (867m)
Garbh Bheinn

MAPS: Harvey's Walker's Map
& Superwalker Glen Coe, OS
Outdoor Leisure 38 Ben Nevis
& Glen Coe, OS Landranger 41
Ben Nevis, Fort William and
surrounding area

REFRESHMENTS:
Kinlochleven and Glen Coe
village have cafes, chip shops
and bars

ADVICE:
No real problems on this steep
short climb though the terrain
is rugged

After a brief stroll to the shores of beautiful Loch Leven a short but steep climb up rough slopes leads to the impressive pointed peak of Garbh Bheinn, a superb viewpoint.

A   Caolasnacon and Loch Leven   132 612

Loch Leven is a magnificent sea loch, stretching some 8 miles (13km) from the Ballachulish Bridge, beyond which it merges with Loch Linnhe, to Kinlochleven. Fjord-like in nature, a narrow thread of water hemmed in by steep mountains, at a glance it seems more like an inland loch than an arm of the sea. The name given to the thin neck of water where the walk starts is Caolas nan Con, which means the Narrows of the Dog. Here the loch is squeezed tight between the rocky knoll of Torr Phioda on the south side and the final rock outcrops of Beinn na Caillich on the north side. This section was a problem for shipping when boats were the main means of transport to and from the Aluminium Works in Kinlochleven (the road was only built in 1922) and had to be regularly dredged.

Loch Leven is rich in wildlife. Graceful mute swans are often seen, floating calmly on the loch or grazing on the shore (they eat grass), sometimes with cygnets as they nest by the loch.

Mute Swan on Loch Leven at Caolasnacon

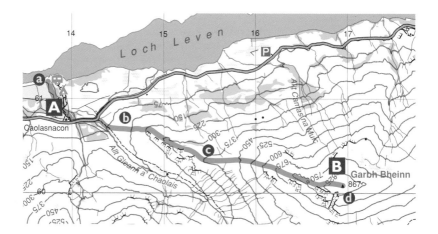

Cormorants feed in the loch too. Guessing where they will reappear after they dive is an interesting game to play. It's surprising just how far they can go in one dive. You may see seals too, their heads bobbing up to look round, a reminder that this is the sea, however much like an inland water it may look. At low water the seaweed-covered rocks give this away too.

There is an excellent campsite at Caolasnacon in a beautiful situation right on the edge of the loch.

a   Before starting the climb a stroll can be made down to the shores of Loch Leven near the camp site on the west side of the burn. Once on the shore you can walk along the pebble

Garbh Bheinn

beach ¼ mile (400m) or so. Garbh Bheinn looks massive from here, a great bulk of a hill, foreshortened by its nearness. Small crags reach down to the water on the far side of the loch, only 100 yards (91m) away. Just above these the banks are thick with deciduous trees, a wonderful sight in autumn sunlight when they glow yellow, orange and red.

b   The ascent of Garbh Bheinn begins on the east side of the bridge over the Allt Gleann a'Chaolais where a rough path heads up beside the burn. After 50 yards (45m) or so an indistinct path cuts up eastwards onto the west ridge of Garbh Bheinn. It's easy to miss this path, a birch sapling hides the start. If you do, simply head up the slopes to the ridge anywhere during the first kilometre or so. The lower slopes are richly vegetated with heather, bracken and small birch trees which have to be pushed through and which can leave you soaked from the hips down when they are wet with rain or dew.

c   The ridge is now followed to the summit over a series of false tops. A path appears from time to time including a rudimentary path on the rocky spine between 1,800–2,300ft (550–700m) there are many rock outcrops and near the top a narrowish section of sloping quartzite slabs, but the climb isn't difficult, just steep. During the ascent the views of the surrounding hills open up. The long undulating high level crest of the Mamores can be seen clearly over Loch Leven. Just to the south the little-visited north side of the Aonach Eagach (see Walk 29) comes into sight. Below to the right several small waterfalls can be seen on the Allt Gleann a'Chaolais while across the glen a fine waterslide comes down a prominent ravine on the north-east slopes of Meall Garbh, an outlying spur of the Aonach Eagach.

B   Garbh Bheinn 169 601
From the summit the views of the Mamores with the bulk of Ben Nevis rising behind them and the Aonach Eagach are superb while to the east the long line of the Blackwater Reservoir can be seen (see Walk 8). The nearest other summit is Meall Dearg, the second highest peak on the Aonach Eagach and 1 mile (1.6km) or so to the south-west. The ground only drops to 1,725ft (525m) between the two summits but this drop and it's height (2,845ft/867m) are more than enough to make Garbh Bheinn a Corbett (see note on Mam na Gualainn in Walk 9).

Because of the link via a high col Garbh Bheinn can be regarded as an outlier of Meall Dearg. It certainly has the

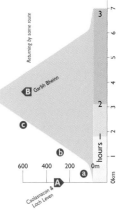

Please note: time taken calculated according to Naismith's Formula (see p.2)

Garbh Bheinn (foreground) with
Ben Nevis in the background

appropriate ruggedness for a connection with the Aonach
Eagach. Indeed, the name means rough hill. There are two
other Garbh Bheinns within 15 miles (24km) of Ben Nevis,
one of which is the better known Ardgour Garbh Bheinn, and
a fourth further away. It's surprising that there aren't far more
in the Western Highlands as there are certainly dozens if not
hundreds of hills that the description fits.

Despite its isolated position Garbh Bheinn doesn't stand out
in many views as there are usually other higher hills beyond
it. Perhaps the best viewpoint is beside the B863 road on the
north side of Loch Leven near Rubha Cladaich (GR 128 610)
from where you can look straight up the west ridge.

Garbh Bheinn belongs to Kinlochleven though the relationship
is not a happy one, as the hill towers over the town and during
the winter totally blocks the sun from houses on the south
side of the River Leven. The hill also has a literary connection
as the heroes of Robert Louis Stevenson's *Kidnapped*, Alan
Breck and David Balfour, hid on its northern slopes after
fleeing from Glen Coe.

d There are two options for the descent. The first is to
retrace your steps down the ridge, perhaps opting for a steep
descent of the southern slopes at some point to the path in
Gleann a'Chaolais below. The rocks can be slippery so do take
care. If transport can be arranged or you don't mind the 3
mile (5km) road walk back to Caolasnacon you can descend
the pathless broad north-east ridge down to the West
Highland Way ½ mile (800m) or so from Kinlochleven.

SGORR A'CHOISE & MEALL MOR

T hese two small hills give superb views of their much bigger neighbours, especially Beinn a'Bheithir, as well as Loch Leven and Glen Coe. Much of the walk is on rough pathless terrain and there is one steep climb.

A   Ballachulish Tourist Information Centre   083 583

Ballachulish is an old slate mining village with a growing number of attractions for visitors. There is a large car park outside the Information Centre. As well as the usual tourist material the centre has an interesting display on the slate industry.

a   From the car park walk past the Information Centre, and take the road that runs south-west through Ballachulish past a supermarket and some playing fields. Follow this road for 550 yards (500m) to where it turns west and crosses the river Laroch. Immediately across the bridge turn left up a minor road, signposted 'Public Footpath to Glen Creran', that climbs past a church and the primary school out of the village and into Gleann an Fhiodh.

b   The road becomes a farm track and then a path that traverses the lower slopes of Beinn a'Bheithir high above the west bank of the River Laroch.

B   Gleann an Fhiodh   078 560

The soaring pyramid of Sgorr a'Choise can be seen clearly from the walk up Gleann an Fhiodh. On the east bank of the river Laroch lies a large conifer plantation above which rise the slopes of Meall Mor.

START/FINISH:
Information Centre, Ballachulish. Gaelicbus from Fort William

DISTANCE: 9 miles (15km)

APPROXIMATE TIME: 6–8 hours

HIGHEST POINT: 2,217ft (676m) Meall Mor

MAPS:
OS Outdoor Leisure 38 Ben Nevis & Glen Coe, OS Landranger 41 Ben Nevis, Fort William and surrounding area

REFRESHMENTS:
Cafes and bars in Ballachulish

ADVICE:
Steep sections, no path in places

Sgorr a'Choise

On the summit of Sgorr a'Choise

c The path crosses a number of small streams running down from Beinn a'Bheithir. The biggest of these is the Allt Sheileach, along the steep banks of which there is an attractive ribbon of birch trees out of reach of the destructive browsing of sheep and deer. Once across this stream the path approaches the River Laroch.

d Leave the path about ⅔ mile (1km) beyond the Allt Sheileach, cross the River Laroch, here just a small burn, and climb the steep, heather-clad slopes to the east to the knobbly south-west ridge of Sgorr a'Choise. The remnants of the old boundary fence on the slopes of Sgorra'Choise are an aid to navigation to the top.

e The narrow rocky ridge, dotted with pale quartzite, leads to the neat little summit of Sgorr a'Choise.

C Sgorr a'Choise 084 551

Sgorr a'Choise, although only 2,217ft (676m) high, has a real mountain feel about it. Perched above steep rocky slopes the airy summit is a fine viewpoint for the surrounding area. Directly west lies Beinn a'Bheithir with its huge east face towering above Gleann an Fhiodh and long sharp ridges running north towards Loch Leven and the tiny houses of Ballachulish. To the north-east the jagged crest of the Aonach Eagach rises above the rounded swelling of nearby Meall Mor. The massive buttresses of Bidean nam Bian soar into the sky to the east with to the south of it a mass of smaller peaks around Sgor na h-Ulaidh. Directly southwards dark forested Glen Creran splits the mountain cluster. West of this glen stands Fraochaidh, at 2,883ft (879m) much smaller than the

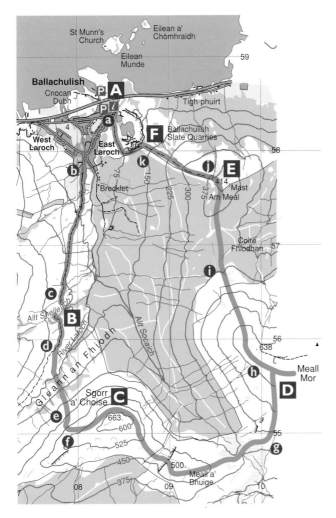

mountains to the north and east, but still impressive due to its isolated situation. Away beyond this peak, distinct but distant, Ben More on Mull and the Paps of Jura can be seen.

f   Descend the broad south-east ridge which runs above two plantation filled corries to a minor top, Meall a'Bhuige, then turns north-east to a boggy col just above the trees. Most of the walking is on rough tussocky slopes but immediately below the summit of Sgorr a'Choise the ridge is steep and rocky. The easiest way down is to go south for 109 yards (100m) or so and then cut back east to the ridge.

Sgorr a'Choise (left) and Beinn a'Bheithir from Meall Mor

g Easy angled grassy slopes lead north from the col to Meall Mor. The large summit cairn stands on a long though not very high rock outcrop, the only distinguishing feature on this rounded hill which has none of the mountain atmosphere of Sgorr a'Choise.

D Meall Mor 106 559

Meall Mor makes up the westernmost portion of the National Trust for Scotland's Glencoe estate. The name means Big Hill, a reference, presumably, to the large area the hill covers and also its low height as 'Meall' means a hill rather than a mountain. It's an excellent viewpoint for U-shaped Glen Coe, which stretches away to the east between huge mountain walls. There's also a good view back to the rugged pyramid of Sgorr a'Choise with Beinn a'Bheithir beyond it.

h Although Ballachulish lies only 2 miles (3.2km) away as the crow flies, reaching it is not that simple as a vast sweep of dense plantations lies in the way. These are best crossed at their narrowest point which lies to the north-west of Meall Mor. Firstly though the route is retraced along the rock escarpment and then the broad grassy north-west shoulder descended towards the trees. As you go down these slopes aim for the break in the trees that can be seen running north towards a communications mast near the summit of Am Meall. A high deer fence surrounds the forest. Look out for the small gate through this. It's half the height of the fence, which runs over the top of it.

i Once in the plantation follow the break in the trees, in which there runs a broken down drystone wall, down to a col where there is a larger open space. The gap in the trees ahead will take you to the northern edge of the plantation but it does involve a bit of bushwhacking when it fades away. It's easier to turn right (east) for a few hundred yards to where another break in the trees heads north to come out near the communications mast. There's no gate in the high fence here but a stout set of posts and crossbars that looks as though it should be a gate makes climbing it relatively simple.

j   Once across the fence turn north-west and follow a path across some boggy ground to a stile over another fence and then down beside the edge of the plantation.

E   Am Meall
This little hill, just 1,358ft (414m) high, is a superb viewpoint for Loch Leven and the mountains to the west. During the descent you look straight down the loch to the Ballachulish bridge, Loch Linnhe and the mountains of Ardgour. The village of Ballachulish lies directly below.

k   At the lower edge of the forest the path turns left to avoid the old slate quarries, which lie straight ahead, and then curves round past the quarries to come out opposite the Information Centre.

F   Ballachulish Slate Quarries
Slate was first worked in Ballachulish in 1694 and quarrying only ceased in 1955. It was an important industry, employing around 2,000 people in the mid-nineteenth century, and the reason for the development of the village. Today the quarry floor has been grassed over and the spoil heaps removed. Placid pools lie beneath the tiers of slate and the noise, dust and dirt of the industry has gone.

Loch Leven from Am Meall

SGORR NA CICHE (THE PAP OF GLENCOE)

START/FINISH:
Glencoe village. Gaelicbus from Fort William

DISTANCE:
5 miles (8km)

APPROXIMATE TIME:
2½–4 hours

HIGHEST POINT:
2,435ft (742m)

MAPS:
Harvey's Walker's Map Superwalker Glen Coe, OS Outdoor Leisure 38 Ben Nevis & Glen Coe, OS Landranger 41 Ben Nevis, Fort William and surrounding area

REFRESHMENTS:
Glen Coe village; hotel on A82

ADVICE:
The climb is steep and rough and the route isn't that obvious in places so although the walk is only short and the hill is relatively small, full hillwalking skills and equipment are needed

Sgorr na Ciche is one of the most distinctive hills in the region, rising abruptly from the shores of Loch Leven. The views from the summit are magnificent, making the steep ascent well worthwhile. Even more than most this is definitely a peak for a clear day.

a   The walk starts in Glencoe village. Cross the stone bridge over the River Coe and follow the old road up the glen. The woods lining the road are quite impressive with some large beech and oak and one huge Scots pine. Alders grow in marshy areas near the river. In a couple of places the road can be left for short footpaths through the woods between the road and river.

View down the River Coe to Sgorr nam Fiannaidh from the bridge in Glencoe village

b   Half a mile (800m) from the village the dense forest on the left ends and a tarmac track, signposted for Laraichean, heads up the hillside. Our route follows the next, unmetalled, track, just a few yards further on. Where this track forks a few hundred yards up the hillside take the right branch across a burn. The track now traverses across the hillside to end at a dam on the next burn, the Allt a'Mhuillinn. The name means Stream of the Mill and is common in the Highlands as many streams were used to power mills. A better known Allt a'Mhuillinn is the one below the great north cliffs of Ben Nevis (see Walk 30). Highland cattle are grazed on the hillside here and you may pass some of these shaggy, long-haired beasts as you climb. You may also curse them as you plod stickily through the muddy morass they've made of the track.

c   On the far side of the Allt a'Mhuillinn, which runs down a narrow gully, take the path which ascends directly up the hillside. In places this path is very muddy and slippery, especially after heavy rain, though this is more of a problem in descent, when you can find yourself flat on your back as your feet shoot from under you unless you're careful, than in ascent. At a height of about 1,000ft (300m) the path cuts right, away from the burn, in a long zigzag. Soon after it turns back towards the gully, the path divides. Keep straight on here (the left fork); the right branch heads for Sgorr nam Fiannaidh at the east end of the Aonach Eagach. The path finishes on the col between Sgorr na Ciche and Sgorr nam Fiannaidh. If you lose the path at any time simply follow the line of the Allt a'Mhuillinn to the col.

d   The final slopes of Sgorr na Ciche rise steeply above the col. A short, easy scramble over quartzite scree and boulders, slippery when wet, leads to the summit. Alternatively there is a path just a little further round to the north that avoids any scrambling.

A   Sgorr na Ciche   125 594

Because of its position between Glen Coe and Loch Leven the views from Sgorr na Ciche are wonderful, among the best in the region. Below to the east the long narrow fjord of Loch Leven stretches out with the unbroken high level line of the Mamores on the skyline above it. Round to the west is the Ballachulish bridge with the long, sweeping, graceful ridges of Beinn a'Bheithir (see Walk 23) running down towards it from the south and the more distant peaks of Ardgour rising beyond it in the west. Turning to look up Glen Coe massive, many-peaked Bidein nam Bian (see Walk 24) dominates the view.

The prominent summit cone of Sgorr na Ciche, whose shape gives the peak its name, is made of hard, erosion-resistant, quartzite, hence the pointed shape. Similar quartzite capped peaks can be found in the Mamores and the Grey Corries (see Walks 17, 18 and 20). Sgorr na Ciche is visible from many points. One of the best views is from the shores of Loch Leven between Ballachulish and Glencoe village. The peak is also prominent in the view down Loch Leven from the slopes around Mamore Lodge at the eastern end of the loch. (See Walk 4).

Sgorr na Ciche is classified as a Graham, that is a Scottish hill between 2,000 and 2,500ft (6,560–8,200m) high with a re-ascent to any adjacent higher hill of at least 500ft (1640m). Compared with the Munros and Corbetts this is a recent list, first compiled in 1992 and named for the late Fiona Graham. There are 224 Grahams in total.

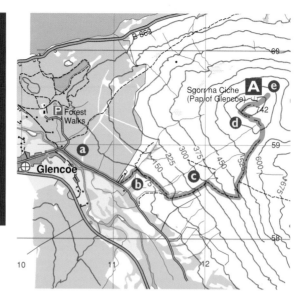

Sgorr na Ciche rising above Glencoe village

In legend the slopes of Sgorr na Ciche, like many places in the Highlands and throughout Ireland, are associated with the great mythical Celtic hero Fingal or Finn mac Cumhaill and his warrior people the Feinne, who are celebrated in the poems of the bard Ossian, Fingal's son. The Feinne were attacked by King Earragan of Lochlann (Scandinavia) whose fleet had sailed up Loch Leven. To defend themselves the Feinne dug four large ditches on the hillside below Sgor nam Fiannaidh (which means the Peak of the Feinne) and Sgorr na Ciche. They then took stones from Sgorr na Ciche to fling at the invaders. There is also an Ossian's Cave high on the cliff face of Aonach Dubh, one of the Three Sisters of Glen Coe and a shoulder of Bidein nam Bian, where Ossian is meant to have lived in the fifth century. This seems highly unlikely as the cave, a long black slot clearly visible from the floor of the glen, can only be reached by a 200ft (60m) difficult and dangerous rock climb. Also, the floor of the cave slopes at an angle of 45°.

Sgorr na Ciche lies at the western end of a long ridge that runs east for some 6 miles (10km) to the Devil's Staircase and which includes the narrow, rocky crest of the Aonach Eagach (see Walk 29). The name means the steep, pointed peak of the breast or nipple, Ciche being the genitive form of Cioch, a breast. This is a common mountain name in the Highlands, past inhabitants having no inhibitions about naming peaks for body parts. The hill is often called the Pap of Glencoe, which means the same, Pap being a Scots word that also means breast. It comes from a Norse root and has, according to Peter Drummond (*Scottish Hill and Mountain Names*), northern English links.

e　There are two options for the descent. The first is to return by the ascent route. The alternative, if transport back to Glen Coe can be arranged or you don't mind a 2½ mile (4km) road walk at the end of the day, is to descend the north-east ridge to the B863 road beside Loch Leven.

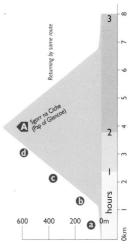

Please note: time taken calculated according to Naismith's Formula (see p.2)

LAIRIG EILDE & LAIRIG GARTAIN

START/FINISH:
Upper Glen Coe. There are small parking places near The Study. The Citylink/Skye-Ways Glasgow to Skye and Edinburgh to Skye buses go through Glen Coe and may let passengers off near the head of the glen

DISTANCE:
9 miles (14.5km)

APPROXIMATE TIME:
4–6 hours

HIGHEST POINT:
1,575ft (480m)

MAPS:
Harvey's Walker's Map & Superwalker Glen Coe, OS Outdoor Leisure 38 Ben Nevis & Glen Coe, OS Landranger 41 Ben Nevis, Fort William and surrounding area

REFRESHMENTS:
Kingshouse Hotel. Various establishments in Lower Glen Coe

ADVICE: There are several streams to cross on this walk which can be dangerous when in spate so this is a walk best done in dry weather. In high season you may wish to begin the walk at the Lairig Gartain as The Study can become very congested

The circuit of these two passes, which lie either side of the long ridge of the Buachaille Etive Beag, takes the walker through magnificent mountain scenery. There is a path the whole way but it can be wet and muddy and it is steep and rough in places, making this walk just as difficult as many summits.

A The Study 182 564

Although the name Glen Coe is usually applied to the whole area from Kingshouse and the head of Glen Etive to Loch Leven the glen really begins at The Study. Here the River Coe runs through a rocky gorge into which the Allt Lairig Eilde plunges in a fine 65ft (20m) waterfall. Part of the fall is trapped in a deep groove; the other part spreads out over the rocks. The actual Study is a flat-topped rock situated beside the old road, some 100ft (30m) above the A82. The name has nothing to do with study but is a corruption of the Scots word 'Stiddie', meaning an anvil, itself a translation of the more evocative Gaelic name, Innean a'Cheathaich, the Anvil of the Mist.

The classic view of Glen Coe is from The Study. The ragged ridge of the Aonach Eagach runs down the northern side of the glen but the eye is drawn to the famous Three Sisters, Beinn Fhada, Gearr Aonach and Aonach Dubh. These massive buttresses of dark rock were formed when the glacier that carved out Glencoe sliced off the ends of three spurs running

Signpost in Glen Etive

out from Bidean nam Bian (see Walk 24). The tiny distant summit of Bidean can be seen between Beinn Fhada and Gearr Aonach. It is a spectacular scene, only marred by the busy A82 running down the heart of the glen. It's a pity this road wasn't built along the line of the first military roads, over the Devil's Staircase to Kinlochleven. Glen Coe is not the place for a busy trunk road.

Stob Coire Sgreamhach and the Allt Coire Eilde

a From The Study walk up the A82 a few hundred yards to where a Scottish Rights of Way Society signpost by a large cairn points the way to the Lairig Eilde.

b The path crosses boggy hillside and enters the Allt Lairig Eilde glen, crossing the burn. There is no bridge and the ford can be dangerous when the river is in spate. I've been here after a day of heavy rain when the stream was a foaming torrent of white water, swirling round in dark pools and boiling up in clouds of spray over hidden boulders, a spectacular sight but one to look at only and not venture into. If in any doubt, don't attempt the crossing. Instead, you could continue up the left (true right) bank (there are bits of a path in places) for a little over a mile (1.6km) to where the path recrosses the river.

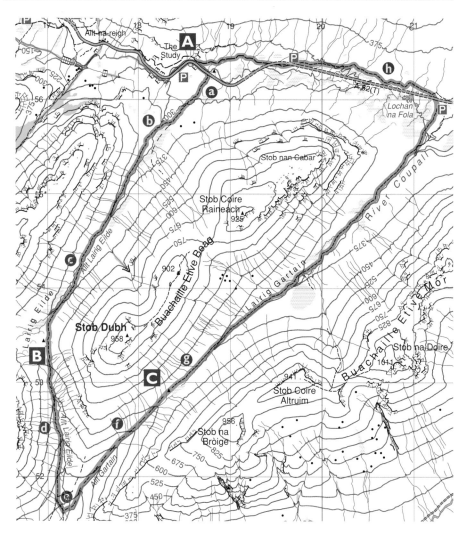

c If the crossing is feasible follow the boggy path up the glen, recrossing the burn about a ⅓ mile (500m) before the top of the pass at 1,575ft (480m), some 830ft (250m) higher than the start.

B Lairig Eilde 161 534

The Allt Lairig Eilde runs between the two long parallel ridges of the Buachaille Etive Beag and Beinn Fhada. The pass itself is a broad saddle situated dramatically between the peaks at the southern ends of these ridges, 3,130ft (958m) Stob Dubh and 3,497ft (1,070m) Stob Coire Sgreamhach, both classified as Munros. Stob Dubh rises very steeply above the pass but it does look possible, if arduous, to climb it from here. Stob Coire Sgreamhach on the other hand presents a very rugged, rocky face to the pass, up which it looks as if it would be very difficult to climb. If you want to ascend Stob Dubh it's easier to do so from lower down the Allt Lairig Eilde by the first ford. From here you can climb to the low point on Buachaille Etive Beag and walk the ridge to Stob Dubh with excellent views all around. Just above the col to the north-east and easily climbed from here is another Munro, 3,034ft (925m) Stob Coire Raineach.

Lairig Eilde means the Pass (Lairig) of the Hinds and there's a good chance that you'll see red deer on this walk. You may not see much other wildlife however, except maybe for dippers on the stream, ptarmigan on the rocky slopes and, if you're lucky, a golden eagle soaring far overhead, because, like most of the Glen Coe region (and indeed the Highlands as a whole), the forest that once cloaked the lower glen and provided food and shelter for birds and animals is long gone. Over-grazing by deer and sheep prevents any regeneration and keeps the land boggy and impoverished. The reason trees are often only to be found along the steep banks of streams and deep inside gorges is because grazing animals cannot reach them here not because, as is sometimes claimed, it's the only place they can grow. It is a shame that the National Trust for Scotland, who own this land, do not do much more to control grazing and allow the forest to return.

d From the pass the path drops to the south down a steeper, narrower glen on the west bank of a stream that is again called Allt Lairig Eilde. It's only about a mile (1.6km) down to a height of only 245ft (90m) at Dalness in Glen Etive where another Scottish Rights of Way Society signpost points the way up to the Lairig Gartain as well as back to the Lairig Eilde.

e There's no need to descend all the way into Glen Etive however. At about 600ft (185m) the first of several paths forks off left to cross the stream and curve round the lower slopes of Stob Dubh into the glen of the Allt Gartain. Where you cross the Allt Lairig Eilde there are good views up to a series of waterfalls pouring down the rocky streambed and below to a small, wooded gorge.

f Beyond the Allt Lairig Eilde the path up the steep southern nose of Stob Dubh – an arduous way up

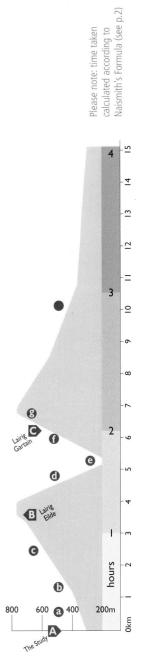

unrelentingly steep slopes – is crossed. Once over this path contour round to the Allt Gartain and then climb the steep slopes to the col, which again is at 1,575ft (480m). The path to the pass is intermittent but the way is very clear.

C   Lairig Gartain 183 521

The Lairig Gartain is a classic example of a glaciated valley. The perfect 'U' shape is seen well from lower Glen Etive with the towering cones of Stob na Broige and Stob Dubh, the south-western peaks of the Buachailles Etive Mor and Etive Beag (the Big and Little Herdsmen of Etive), rising on either side. Both mountains can be climbed from the Lairig Gartain but this is best done from the River Coupall glen a bit further on where steep slopes lead to the low points on each ridge.

Gartain means an enclosed field though the pass could be named for somebody as Gartan is a personal name.

g Beyond the top of the pass the path improves as it runs along the west bank of the River Coupall in wide, boggy glen. At the foot of the glen the path crosses even boggier ground, fords the burn running out of Lochan na Fola and reaches the A82 at its high point.

h Fast traffic along the A82 makes it dangerous for walkers so rather than follow it back to the start cross it and take the old road just beyond the far side. This makes for a more pleasant walk too. Apart from one brief return to the A82 where it crosses then recrosses the old road the latter can be followed all the way back to The Study.

The Lairig Gartain between Buchaille Etive Beag and Buchaille Etive Mor

BEINN A'CHRULAISTE

/ ❖ ❦ ⚶

START/FINISH:
Altnafeadh, Upper Glen Coe.
The Citylink/Skye-Ways
Glasgow to Skye and
Edinburgh to Skye buses go
through Glen Coe and may let
passengers off near the head
of the glen

DISTANCE:
6 miles (10km)

APPROXIMATE TIME:
4–5 hours

HIGHEST POINT:
2,811ft (857m)

MAPS:
Harvey's Walker's Map &
Superwalker Glen Coe, OS
Outdoor Leisure 38 Ben Nevis
& Glen Coe, OS Landranger 41
Ben Nevis, Fort William and
surrounding area

REFRESHMENTS:
Kingshouse Hotel. Various
places in Lower Glen Coe

ADVICE:
Although not a difficult climb
there are no paths so
navigation can be difficult in
poor visibility. A large scale
map will show positions of
fences and may provide
additional help. Access to the
Black Corries Estate is
discouraged in the stalking
season; for access call 01855
851272. For further discussion
of access issues see
Introduction pp.11–12)

Like many isolated, lower hills Beinn a'Chrulaiste is a superlative viewpoint, especially for the cliffs of Buachaille Etive Mor. The walk can be done either way round and started at either Altnafeadh or Kingshouse. Clockwise from Altnafeadh, as described, it gives great views over Rannoch Moor on the descent and the Kingshouse Hotel is available for refreshments before the return to the start. Going the other way there are good views of the Glen Coe hills from the descent.

A Altnafeadh 222 563

Altnafeadh is a former resting place or stance for cattle drovers taking their herds south after the difficult crossing of the 1,800 foot (550m) high pass above Kinlochleven. There is a good view of the west ridge of Beinn a'Chrulaiste, which is our ascent route, just south of the A82. The name, properly Allt nam Feith, means Burn of the Bogs. Across the road from the buildings the West Highland Way sets off through the edge of a small conifer wood to Kinlochleven by way of the series of zigzags known as the Devil's Staircase. This is the line of Caulfield's military road to Fort William, which we also come across in Walks 4 and 9.

a From Altnafeadh go up the Devil's Staircase track to the top of the trees and turn right following the fence at the top edge of the wood. Cross the stream and go to the corner where the new fence meets the wood. Climb the fence and go through the gate immediately to the right. Turn left and follow the fence (on your left-hand side) up hill to another gate in the fence you have been following. This is a very wet and boggy section. At the gate go through and immediately climb over the fence on your right-hand side. You are now on open hillside. You may pick up a faint path which meanders up the ridge.

b The route up the west ridge crosses a minor top, 2,095ft (639m) Stob Beinn a'Chrulaiste, then climbs steadily to the summit. The walking is over rough ground but the only crags are to the south. There isn't a path but as long as you stick to the broad crest of the ridge there should be no difficulties.

B Beinn a'Chrulaiste 246 567

Beinn a'Chrulaiste means Rocky Hill. However, although the hill does have some small cliffs and is quite stony, the name suits it less than it does most of the hills lying just to the west. And

Beinn a'Chrulaiste

the real rocky hill hereabouts is the one that can be seen looking magnificent to the south-west, Buachaille Etive Mor (see Walk 25). Stob Dearg, the northernmost summit of this long mountain, rises up as a tremendous rough and rugged pointed peak above a huge wall of rock, a wall that, on closer examination, is seen to be split into great buttresses, ridges and deep gullies.

Whilst Buachaille Etive Mor dominates the view there is much more to see. For the best scene walk around the rim of the quite large flat summit area as the views are better from the edges. Further round to the west the peaks of Bidean nam Bian stand out while to the north-west the long undulating line of the Mamores is visible with the bulky top of Ben Nevis rising above it. Out to the east the flat expanse of Rannoch Moor, sparkling with lochans and burns, stretches away into the distance. Of the hills rising beyond it the pointed peak that stands out is called Schiehallion. There are masses more hills in view and fun

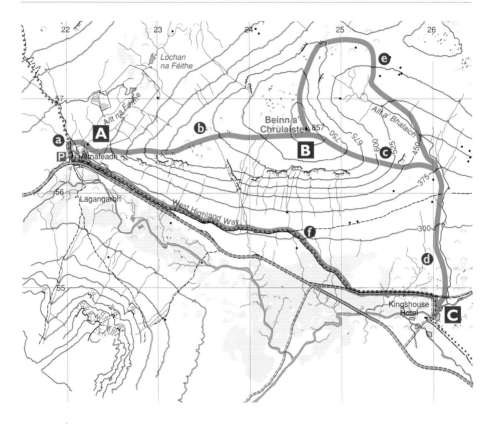

can be had (and time taken!) trying to identify them all.

Beinn a'Chrulaiste is classified as a Corbett, that is a peak in Scotland between 2,500 (762m) and 3,000ft (915m) with a drop of 500ft (152m) between it and the nearest higher hill.

c   The descent could be made by the same route but a circular route is more enjoyable than an out and back one so I'd recommend going down the east ridge. The first short section is south-east round the rim of Coire Bhalach then due east down rugged slopes with occasional little rock outcrops to the Allt a'Bhalaich (the burn of the pass – a bealach is a high mountain pass).

d At the stream turn right (south) and follow it down to the Black Corries estate road just east of its junction with the road to the Kingshouse Hotel. For refreshments turn left here and take this road over an arched stone bridge to the Hotel. To return to the start without visiting the Hotel keep straight on (See f below).

e An alternative, longer descent route is by the north-east ridge. This curves east at a height of 2,215ft (675m) and descends to a col from where a further descent can be made south to the Allt a'Bhalaich in Coire Bhalach. For an even longer walk you could continue from the col to the twin rounded tops of Meall Bhalach (2,322ft/708m and 2,312ft/705m) before descending into Coire Bhalach.

C   The Kingshouse Hotel 259 544

The Kingshouse Hotel is an old coaching inn, dating back to the 1750s, as well as a former cattle drovers stance like Altnafeadh. In the eighteenth and nineteenth centuries the innkeeper not only paid no rent but also had a government grant because of the need for somewhere offering food and shelter for travellers in such a remote, uninhabited region on the edge of Rannoch Moor. The service offered was basic and minimal however. William and Dorothy Wordsworth came here in 1803 and Dorothy wrote in her journal: 'Never did I see such a miserable, such a wretched place … the floors far dirtier than an ordinary house could be if it were never washed.' Supper was no better: 'a shoulder of mutton so hard that it was impossible to chew the little flesh that might be scraped off the bones, and some sorry soup made of barley and water, for it had no other taste.' Thirty-eight years later in 1841 Charles Dickens found things somewhat improved and had 'a very hearty meal'. Today the Hotel is popular with mountaineers intent on climbs on Buachaille Etive Mor in both summer and winter, walkers doing the West Highland Way, which passes the door, and, when its snowy, skiers using the nearby White Corries downhill ski slopes.

f   The West Highland Way leads from the Kingshouse back to Altnafeadh. Start by retracing your steps back to the junction with the Black Corries road. Here turn left and follow the road past some old ruins, the remains of the long abandoned Queenshouse, another inn built in the eighteenth century, to where the old military road, signposted for the West Highland Way, turns off to the right just before the A82 is reached. This track leads back to the start across the lower slopes of Beinn a'Chrulaiste with good views over the A82 and the River Etive to Buachaille Etive Mor.

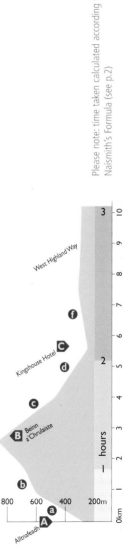

Please note: time taken calculated according to Naismith's Formula (see p.2)

BEINN MAOL CHALUIM

START/FINISH:
Lower Glen Etive. Postbus (Monday to Saturday) to Glen Etive Post Office from Fort William and Glen Coe

DISTANCE:
5 miles (8km)

APPROXIMATE TIME:
4–6 hours

HIGHEST POINT:
2,975ft (907m)

MAPS:
Harvey's Walker's Map & Superwalker Glen Coe, OS Landranger 50 Glen Orchy and surrounding area/41 Ben Nevis, Fort William and surrounding area

REFRESHMENTS:
None in Glen Etive. The Kingshouse Hotel just beyond the head of Glen Etive is the nearest place for refreshments

ADVICE:
Although short this walk involves a rough, steep climb up pathless slopes and so is more arduous than the distance suggests. As there is no path navigation can be difficult in poor visibility

Hidden from Glen Coe by Bidean nam Bian and lying at the end of a long ridge running up from Glen Etive, Beinn Maol Chaluim is a secretive hill, little known and hard to see. However there are good views from its slopes and summit, making the somewhat strenuous ascent worthwhile.

a The biggest difficulty with this walk is starting it. Lower Glen Etive is covered with dense conifer plantations. Fighting through these is not recommended and there are very few paths or tracks through the trees. However there is a short

gap between plantations just north of the road by Lochan Urr (GR 151 491) which gives access to the steep lower slopes of Beinn Maol Chaluim. There are a few parking places by the cattle grid on the road where it leaves the first belt of thick forest (GR 149 497) at the edge of this gap. Before starting you can walk down to Lochan Urr across whose waters there is a superb view of the great pyramids of Buachaille Etive Mor and Buachaille Etive Beag with the perfect U-shaped glaciated valley of the Lairig Gartain between them.

b The knoll immediately above the road is called Creag na Caillich (the Cliff of the Old Woman). Little rock outcrops dot the hillside. These are best turned by following the forest fence that starts just above the cattle grid. At the top edge of the forest turn left and climb to the south ridge of Beinn Maol

The south face of Bidean nam Bian from Beinn Maol Chaluim

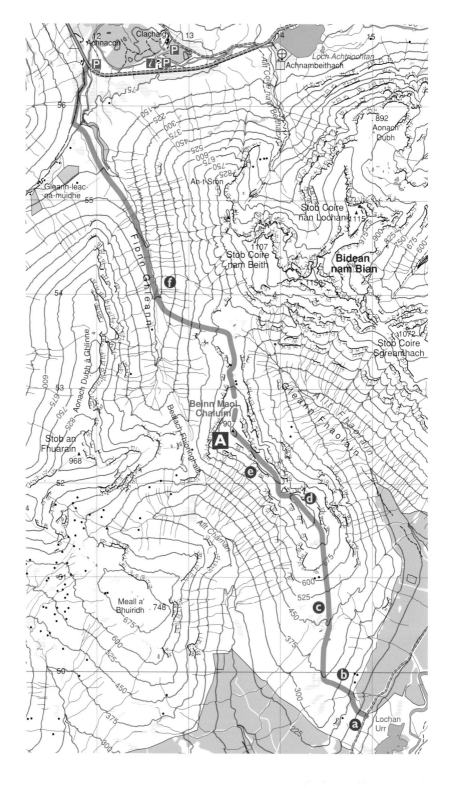

Chaluim. The ground here is covered with big tussocks and long, thick grass. After rain or a heavy dew you can quickly be soaked to the thighs unless waterproof trousers are worn.

c   Once on the broad ridge the angle eases a little but the terrain is still very rough with many small knolls. There's no path so a way has to be picked round the bumps and in and out of shallow dips in the ground. A ½ mile (800m) or so up the ridge broken crags block the way. A scrambling route can be found through these or else they can be bypassed by a traverse rightwards.

d   After another ½ mile (800m) the long summit ridge is reached. This stretches for over ½ mile over several minor tops to the quartzite rocks of the summit. The walking along the fine, narrow ridge is easy (a faint track appears which improves along the ridge) and there are superb views across Gleann Fhaolain to the massive, steep, rocky face of Bidean nam Bian.

A   Beinn Maol Chaluim   135 526

Beinn Maol Chaluim is just 25ft below 3,000ft making it a Corbett rather than a Munro (that is, a peak between 2,500 and 3,000ft rather than a peak over 3,000ft). However it's completely dominated by the much higher and bigger mountain of Bidean nam Bian rising some 800ft (250m) higher less than a mile (1.6km) to the north. Indeed, Beinn Maol Chaluim is linked to Bidean nam Bian by the high pass of the Bealach Fhaolain (2,310ft/705m) and experienced walkers can extend this walk by descending to the bealach then climbing the steep scree above to the ridge of Bidean. The crags that appear to block the way can be turned on the left. Once on the ridge turn right to the 3,772ft (1,150m) summit then continue along the ridge to 3,516ft (1,072m) Stob Coire Sgreamhach, which was promoted to Munro status in the revision of the Tables that took place in 1997. A descent of the south-east slopes of this peak leads down to Dalness in Glen Etive from where it's a 1.2-mile (2-km) walk along the road down the glen back to the start.

There is more to see than Bidean nam Bian however. To the west rise the steep craggy slopes of 3,175ft (968m) Stob an Fhuarain, a subsidiary top of 3,260ft (994m) Sgor na h-Ulaidh, with the long rocky ridge of the Aonach Dubh a'Ghlinne stretching out to the north above the straight line of the Fionn Gleann. Turning south there is a good view across Glen Etive to Ben Starav and its adjacent peaks (see Walks 27

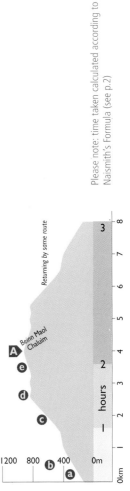

Beinn Maol Chaluim (right foreground) and Bidean nam Bian

and 28) while directly over the glen rise the steep dark slopes of 2,896ft (883m) Stob Dubh.

Beinn Maol Chaluim means Calum's Bare Hill. The Beinn is superfluous as Maol means a bald or bare rounded hill. The name presumably refers to someone called Calum (Malcolm) who was bald though whoever he was and why the hill was named after him has long been forgotten. Was this a jest on behalf of his friends? Did he work or live on the hill? Or did he have an adventure here? No one knows.

e Unless Bidean nam Bian (see above) is climbed too, the best way back to the start is by the ascent route. To the south-west it's a difficult, rocky descent to the Bealach Fhionnghoill and anyway plantations cloak the slopes high up Glen Chaman to the south of the bealach, forcing the walker to skirt round the top of the trees over the south ridge of Beinn Maol Chaluim. The same problem is encountered if you descend to the Bealach Fhaolain and then into Gleann Fhaolain, though this time the walk along the edge of the plantations is longer and over rougher terrain.

f   If transport can be arranged at either end an alternative to returning to the start is to traverse the mountain from Glen Etive to Glen Coe, descending by way of the Fionn Ghleann. The distance is 5 miles (8km). Because of the difficulty in getting down the steep craggy slopes to the Bealach Fhionnghoill at the head of the Fionn Ghleann it's best to go the other way to the Bealach Fhaolain and then down into the Fionn Ghleann. The going in this classic 'V'-shaped glen is quite hard as there are only traces of a path and the ground is rough and tussocky. However there are some attractive waterfalls and cascades on the burn, surrounded, in spring, by rich velvet green vegetation. At the end of the glen the Allt na Muidhe is crossed and the track on the far side followed the short distance to the A82 in Glen Coe about ½ mile (800m) west of the NTS Visitor Centre.

If you spend much time in the hills whatever the weather then you will probably observe various optical phenomena, particularly rainbows. These always appear at what is known as the antisolar point, which is directly opposite the sun. The angle of the sun matters too as the arc of a rainbow always forms at a radius of forty-two degrees around the antisolar point. This is why rainbows are commonly seen late or early in the day or else in autumn or winter when the sun is low in the sky. Rainbows occur when water droplets refract sunlight and are usually seen when a storm has swept past and the sun shines on the wet clouds as they race away. Once you know when and where rainbows are likely to occur you can head for places where you think you will see one. One wet late October day when I wasn't specifically chasing rainbows, as I climbed Beinn Maol Chaluim I noticed occasional hazy flashes of sunlight through the mist in the direction of cloud-shrouded Bidean nam Bian. The mist around me was thinning as I ascended so I hurried up the hill hoping this was a cloud inversion and I would come out of the damp grey blanket that clung to me and perhaps see a rainbow on Bidean. I was right. The summit of the hill was in sunshine and there was a rainbow on the clouds hiding Bidean but it was a beautiful and most strange rainbow as it was white, a perfect white arc shining on the slightly greyer clouds that filled the glen below. All the surrounding hills were swathed in cloud but there was blue sky directly above me and I stood in sunshine, with the white rainbow for company. It was a magical moment, one of those moments that make you shiver with a mixture of awe and pleasure, a moment that tells you again why hills are worth climbing. White rainbows, I learnt later, are very rare (that's the only one I've seen) and are formed when the droplets of water in a cloud are too small to refract the light properly.

BEINN TRILLEACHAN

START/FINISH:
Lower Glen Etive. Postbus (Monday to Saturday) to Glen Etive Post Office from Fort William and Glencoe

DISTANCE:
5 miles (8km)

APPROXIMATE TIME:
5–7 hours

HIGHEST POINT:
2,750ft (839m)

MAPS:
OS Landranger 50 Glen Orchy and surrounding area

REFRESHMENTS:
None in Glen Etive. The Kingshouse Hotel just beyond the head of Glen Etive is the nearest place serving food and drink

ADVICE:
Although short this walk involves a rough, steep climb up pathless slopes and so is more arduous than the distance suggests. As there is no path navigation can be difficult in poor visibility. Steep rocky slopes and cliffs on either side of the summit ridge mean that losing one's way could be very dangerous so this is a walk for a fine day

The long upturned boat shape of Beinn Trilleachan grows increasingly more prominent on the approach down Glen Etive with the smooth and shiny Trilleachan (Etive) Slabs clearly visible. The steep rocky east wall of the hill soars above the upper 3 miles (5km) of Loch Etive. From the long summit ridge there are wonderful views of the surrounding hills, especially Ben Starav directly across the loch. The hill is in a very remote situation and there is a feeling of solitude and spaciousness. It's also a very rocky mountain as can be seen from the mass of hatching on the map. The route described is the easiest way up the hill.

Beinn Trilleachan and the River Etive

a The huge plantation that lines the west side of lower Glen Etive comes to an end where the road reaches the head of the loch. There are a few small spaces where a car can be parked near the forest edge. Although no paths are marked on the map a wet, muddy trail climbs the steep hillside beside the forest fence. This is an old track that connects Glen Etive with Glen Ure and Glen Creran. The walk starts by following this path for a half-mile (800 m) or so until the ground levels off.

b Leaving the path and the forest, turn south-west and climb the slopes above onto the main crest of the hill, which stretches for some 2 miles (3.2km) on to the summit. The first top marked on the map, Meall nan Gobhar (hill of the goat), doesn't really seem to exist on the ground.

c The heavily vegetated and boggy lower slopes give way to more rocky terrain with many small granite knolls appearing. There are many gently angled granite slabs too, which make for easy walking. On the left (east) the ground drops away steeply to Loch Etive and there is a growing feeling of exposure, especially on the 2,515ft (767m) top perched immediately above the huge Trilleachan Slabs (see Walk 7).

d Immediately beyond the Trilleachan Slabs top there is a short but steep and rocky descent down to a col at 2,275ft (693m). The easiest line down to the col is to the right. Beyond the dip more granite slabs lead to the small summit.

Loch Etive and Glen Etive from Beinn Trilleachan

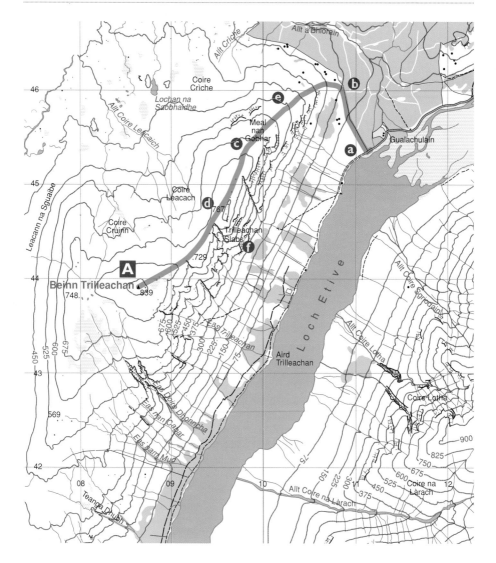

A   Beinn Trilleachan 086 439

The views from the summit are tremendous and extensive. There is a feeling of vast space and wildness, of mountains going on forever. Most impressive is the huge, steep, stream-gorge riven east face of Ben Starav rising straight up to the pointed summit from Loch Etive. On calm days the reflections of this massive mountain wall in the loch are superb. The view back up Glen Etive is excellent too with the twisting, braided river, marshes and meadows at the foot of the glen laid out

Stob Dubh and Stob Coir'an Albannaich from the slopes of Beinn Trilleachan

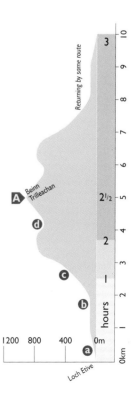

Please note: time taken calculated according to Naismith's Formula (see p.2)

clearly while further away rise the mountains of Glen Coe with Bidean nam Bian and Buachaille Etive Mor particularly prominent. Away down the loch in the other direction the twin peaks of Ben Cruachan rise dramatically into the sky.

Beinn Trilleachan means the Hill of the Sandpiper or Oystercatcher. Either could be correct as both birds, the small bobbing common sandpiper with its distinctive two-note call and the larger black and white oystercatcher with its loud piping call and sharp alarm cry, can be seen and heard on the pebble covered shores of Loch Etive at the base of the mountain. Other birds can be seen on the hill too;. ravens wheeling over the crags and ptarmigan darting about through the boulder fields. In autumn migrant flocks of fieldfares, handsome grey-headed thrushes escaping the Scandinavian winter, travel the lower slopes above the lochside, feeding on rowan and holly berries.

e The easiest and much the safest descent route is to retrace your steps back along the ridge. The wonderful views to the Glen Coe and Blackmount peaks make up for covering the same ground twice.

f For an alternative descent route return to the col below the top of the Trilleachan Slabs from where a wide bouldery gully leads steeply down to the right to the top of a small wood. When the gully begins to open out, turn left to quickly

The Blackmount and the Glen Etive hills from the slopes of Beinn Trilleachan

reach the bottom of the Trilleachan Slabs. Walk 7 describes the route from here.

g It's also possible to continue south-west down the spine of the mountain for a short distance and then find a way down to the loch shore. To attempt this you need good route-finding abilities and confidence in descending steep slopes covered with rocks, boulders and thick vegetation.

RED DEER

The breeding season for red deer is the autumn when the stags enter what is called the rut and their wild roaring and bellowing as they challenge other stags for the hinds can be heard echoing from high corries. It's a wonderfully evocative sound, redolent of untamed nature. I'd been listening to stags roaring at each other across Glen Etive from my camp for a couple of nights before I set off to climb Beinn Trilleachan late one October. Just before the summit a stag with a large rack of antlers appeared only a dozen or so yards away. I paused then carefully approached, using small rock outcrops as cover. The stag seemed oblivious of my presence and I came close enough to notice the strong rank smell and take some photographs. Although powerful and magnificent the beast looked very weary with glazed eyes and a slow tired way of moving so when it finally noted my presence and began to move away I didn't pursue it. Other stags were roaring nearby but it appeared oblivious to them. Perhaps it had been defeated in a fight and had lost all its hinds and was now dejectedly wandering away.

THE GREY CORRIES

This is one of the finest ridge walks in the Highlands, a long high level traverse along a narrow, twisting line of graceful pointed peaks that never drops below 3,350ft (1,020m) and which gives superb views throughout. The Grey Corries (Na Coireachan Leithe in Gaelic) lie between Glen Nevis and Glen Spean and can be seen well from the A82 west of Spean Bridge near the Commando Memorial. The name comes from the vast pale grey screes of quartzite and mica-schist that sweep down from the summits, especially on the northern side of the range. This walk takes the form of a circuit of the great horseshoe that curves round Coire Choimhlidh. Seven peaks are climbed, two of them Munros (separate mountains over 3,000ft/914.4m), the others Tops (subsidiary summits).

a The vast conifer plantations of the Leanachan Forest lie between the A82 road and the Grey Corries. To skirt the dense trees take the minor road from Spean Bridge along the south side of the River Spean to Corriechoille Farm, near which cars can be parked. Fine deciduous woods line this road and there are good views of the rushing river.

START/FINISH:
Corriechoille in Glen Spean.
There are trains and buses to
Spean Bridge

DISTANCE:
12 miles (20km)

APPROXIMATE TIME:
7–9 hours

HIGHEST POINT:
3,860ft (1,177m) Stob Coire
Claurigh

MAPS:
Harvey's Walker's Map &
Superwalker Ben Nevis, OS
Landranger 41 Ben Nevis, Fort
William and surrounding area,
OS Outdoor Leisure 38 Ben
Nevis & Glen Coe (except for
the start)

REFRESHMENTS:
Cafes and bars in Spean Bridge

ADVICE:
Loose scree and narrow ridges.
Some steep sections. Quite
remote

Looking east along the Grey
Corries to Caisteall and Stob
Choire Claurigh

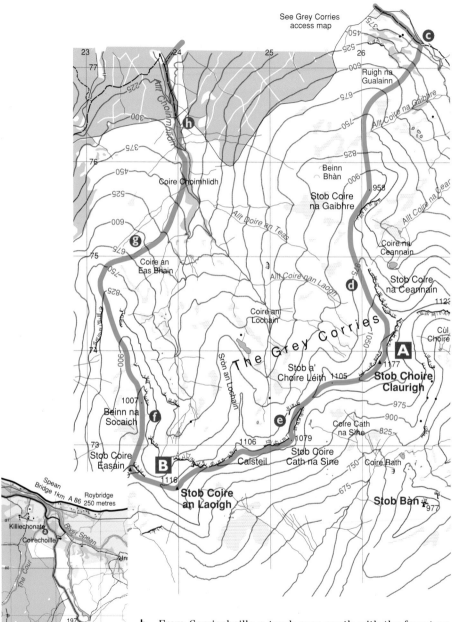

b From Corriechoille a track runs south with the forest on the right and the Allt Leachdach on the left. This is an old drove road that leads up to the Lairig Leacach and then continues on to Kinlochleven, Kingshouse and Rannoch Moor.

Please note: 1km = 0.65cm on this map

Ignore the track going off to the right after about ⅔ mile (1km), this is the return route. After a mile (1.6km) the track crosses the line of an old narrow gauge railway, built to assist with construction of the tunnel taking water from Loch Treig to the east under the mountains to the aluminium works in Fort William. Cars can also be parked just before the railway track.Beyond the old line the track runs through the edge of the forest.

c A few hundred yards after the forest is left the track crosses the Allt Leachdach on a small bridge. Leave the track here and head right up the steep slopes of Ruigh na Gualainn and the eastern arm of the Coire Choimhlidh. Skirt to the left of the rocky outcrop immediately above the bridge, then diagonally right to cross a burn and then pick a suitable route through the rocky outcrops. When the angle eases a little, at around 2,000ft (610m) turn south and follow the broad hillside up to the first summit, 3,142ft (958m) Stob Coire na Gaibhre.

d After a small dip, continue upwards on a rocky ridge that narrows as it climbs with very steep slopes to the east. The lower north top of Stob Choire Claurigh is reached where a spur juts out east to the subsidiary top of Stob Coire na Ceannain. Beyond this summit an easy scramble (avoidable to either side) along a narrow rocky crest leads to the large cairn on Stob Choire Claurigh.

A   Stob Choire Claurigh 262 739

At 3,860ft (1,177m), Stob Choire Claurigh is the highest peak in the Grey Corries. Lying at the east end of the range it gives a superb view along the narrow winding ridge and over the great wild rocky corries lying to the north to the long steep, unbroken east wall of Aonach Mor and Aonach Beag with the big half dome of Ben Nevis rising beyond it. To the east, across the gash of the Lairig Leacach, the bulky twin summits known as the Easains blocks the view. Stob Coire Easain and Stob a'Choire Mheadhoin are regarded as the easternmost summits of the Grey Corries though the low point of 1,653ft (504m) between them and the main group of summits means they are rarely climbed at the same time. Beyond them lies the deep trench of Loch Treig with very different, more rounded, grassier hills, rising on its far side. Across the Water of Nevis to the south the long line of the Mamores stretches into the west. Closer by is the steep pale pyramid of 3,204ft (977m) Stob Ban (White Peak), linked to Stob Choire Claurigh by a 2,656ft (810m) high col. It is possible to go out and back

Please note: time taken calculated according to Naismith's Formula (see p.2)

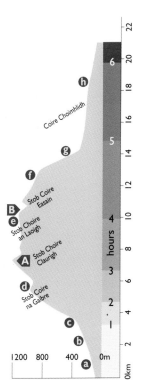

Stob Choire Claurigh from Stob
Coire Cath na Sine

to Stob Ban but you'll need to be fit as the going is steep and rough on quartzite scree and boulders and there is an extra 1,752ft (534m) of ascent.

The meaning of Stob Coire Claurigh isn't clear but it's generally translated as the Peak of the Corrie of Clamouring, from the Gaelic *clamhras*. Drummond (*Scottish Hill and Mountain Names*) points out that bare stony corries like Choire Claurigh greatly amplify noises. A stob is a pointed peak. There are ten stobs in the Grey Corries.

e   From Stob Choire Claurigh the marvellous main ridge of the Grey Corries runs south-west. It looks narrow and rocky and so it is but the walking is surprisingly easy and there's no sense of exposure from the drops either side. The next summit is 3,625ft (1,105m) Stob a'Choire Leith (Peak of the Grey Corrie) soon followed by 3,539ft (1,079m) Stob Coire Cath na Sine (probably Peak of the Corrie of the Battle of the Storm) and then the narrower 3,628ft (1,106m) Caisteal (Castle), so-called because of the battlement-like crags that abut the summit. A spur juts out north from Caisteal, the Sron na Lochain (Nose of the Lochan), between wild high corries. Not far beyond Caisteal the ridge climbs to 3,660ft (1,116m) Stob Coire an Laoigh. When walking in mist it may be helpful to know that there are small cairns on each of the peaks with a large cairn/shelter when you reach Stob Coire an Laoigh.

B Stob Coire an Laoigh 240 725

Stob Coire an Laoigh is the second highest peak in the Grey Corries and the second Munro of the walk. More importantly, it's a superb viewpoint for the Grey Corries to the east as well as west to Aonachs Mor and Beag and Ben Nevis.

The name means the Peak of the Corrie of the Calf, which may mean that cattle were once grazed in the eponymous corrie that lies to the south-east, above the long, wild depths of Coire Rath.

f The next top after Stob Coire an Laoigh is 3,524ft (1,080m) Stob Coire Easain (Peak of the Corrie of the Little Waterfalls) which has the same name as one of the two peaks that rise east of the Lairig Leacach. The main ridge continues south-east to distant Sgurr Choinnich Mor (see Walk 20) but it's a very long way back to the start from there so instead of going on turn north here and leave the ridge for the spur running out to 3,302ft (1,007m) Beinn na Socaich, which is only a tiny bump on a long ridge that runs down to the forest to the north.

g Descend the ridge until past the crags to the east (about 1 mile/1.6km) then leave it to drop north-east down grassy slopes into Coire Choimhlidh and follow the burn to the edge of the forest.

h There is a small dam on the burn where it runs into the forest. There are forest rides both sides of the burn. The one on the east side leads to a clearing where the disused railway ran. This can be followed north-east to the track from the start. The ride west of the burn leads through the forest to join a number of tracks. All those running to the right (north-east) lead back to the track the walk began on.

THE RING OF STEALL

START/FINISH:
Glen Nevis road end. There is a summer bus service from Fort William to the Lower Falls in Glen Nevis, just over a mile (1.6km) from the road end

DISTANCE:
8 miles (13km)

APPROXIMATE TIME:
7–10 hours

HIGHEST POINT:
3,605ft (1,099m) Sgurr a'Mhaim

MAPS:
Harvey's Walker's Map & Superwalker Ben Nevis, OS Outdoor Leisure 38 Ben Nevis & Glen Coe, OS Landranger 41 Ben Nevis, Fort William and surrounding area

REFRESHMENTS:
Cafes in lower Glen Nevis, all services in Fort William

ADVICE:
There are two short passages of easy scrambling where a head for heights is required. Some steep sections. Narrow ridges make the walk unsuitable in high winds

This is a particularly fine ridge walk along the crest of the Mamores, a superb line of peaks that make up the southern edge of beautiful Glen Nevis. There are seventeen summits in total, of which ten are Munros. This walk follows the great horseshoe that encloses Coire a'Mhail. At the foot of the corrie the tremendous Steall Waterfall cascades down into Glen Nevis, hence the name The Ring of Steall. There is a superb walk up the Nevis gorge (see Walk 2), followed by a steep climb and then a marvellous high level ridge walk over six summits, four of them Munros. The walk can be done in either direction but in my view clockwise is the best direction for both safety and enjoyment. The area round Steall Waterfall is steep and it's easy to lose your way in descent here, especially if you're tired and it's growing dark. There have been many accidents, some of them fatal, here. A clockwise round means ascending by the falls which greatly diminishes the risk. Also, going anti-clockwise would involve climbing the long and relentlessly steep path up Sgurr a'Mhaim. It is far more enjoyable to descend this path.

a   The walk starts at the car park at the end of the road up Glen Nevis (see Walk 2). Follow the path up the steep-sided and narrow wooded Nevis Gorge, with the river crashing over boulders below, to the sudden surprise of the flat grassy Steall meadows.

View across Glen Nevis to Steall Falls and An Gearanach

b Walk along the river bank to a three-strand wire bridge that leads across the river to a white cottage, a private mountaineering club hut. The confident will edge carefully across the single lower strand, using the other two for balance. For those who are wary of it, when the river is low there is an easy ford just above the bridge where by judicious use of stones you can keep yourft dry. If the river is in spate you may have to use the bridge or turn back. From the crossing continue up the glen under Steall Falls, a long tumbling, sliding fan of water. The Allt Coire a'Mhail has to be forded next. The best place is a few hundred yards below the falls. Continue on under a steep wooded hillside to the next burn, the Allt Coire Chada Chaoruinn.

c Just across the Allt Coire Chada Chaoruinn a good stalkers path climbs to the right into a shallow corrie. At one point a section of this path has been obliterated by a landslip, which has left a deep groove in the hillside. Follow the upper edge of this until the path reappears. After a few hundred yards the path crosses the stream again and then ascends the steep hillside in short tight zigzags. The very steep craggy face at the head of the corrie looks impassable but just below it the path makes a traverse to the right before angling back up the edge of the face and onto the northern end of the summit ridge of 3,220ft (982m) An Gearanach (The Complainer). On this, the first Munro of the walk, the high level walking starts. There are fine views all around but especially across Coire a'Mhaim to the spiny Devil's Ridge and the blunt cone of Sgurr a'Mhaim.

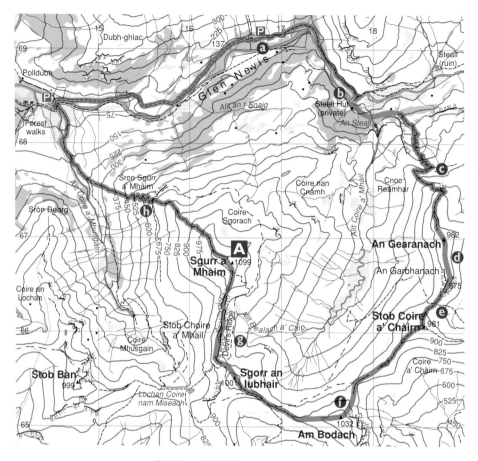

d Beyond An Gearanach the ridge narrows to the thin rocky crest, the top edge of some tilted slabs, of 3,198ft (975m) An Garbhanach, a summit appropriately called the Rough One. The scrambling along this top is fairly easy but quite exposed in places with big drops either side. The hardest of the scrambling can be avoided by paths on the left (east) side.

e More optional scrambling leads steeply down to a col beyond which easier slopes lead to the second Munro, 3,218ft (981m) Stob Coire a'Chairn (Peak of the Corrie of the Cairns), and the main ridge of the Mamores.

f Much easier walking, mostly on grass, leads from Stob Coire a'Chairn down to a col from where the dark, craggy northeast face of 3,385ft (1,032m) Am Bodach (the Old Man), another Munro, towering over Coire na Ba looks quite daunting.

Sgurr a'Mhaim and the Devil's Ridge

The ascent isn't particularly difficult, however, just steep and rocky. This is all a delight, a wonderful walk with splendid views all round. Still on grassy slopes there's another descent to a col from which paths lead down into the corries either side and then up to 3,283ft (1,001m) Sgorr an Iubhair (the Peak of the Yew Tree). This summit was promoted to Munro status in a revision of the list in 1981 then demoted in another revision in 1997, not that it's status matters one jot. Like all the Mamores it's a fine summit in a spectacular situation.

g   At Sgorr an Iubhair the main ridge is left for a bouldery descent to a col below the spur that runs out north to Sgurr a'Mhaim. This spur is known as the Devil's Ridge and consists of a very narrow, rocky arete. There are no real difficulties but the exciting airy scramble is quite exposed in places. The high point of the arete is known as Stob Coire a'Mhail. The most awkward section is at the low point just before the final walk up wide slopes to Sgurr a'Mhaim.

A   Sgurr a'Mhaim 165 667.

At 3,605ft (1,099m) high, Sgurr a'Mhaim is the highest peak and fourth Munro on the walk and the second highest summit in the Mamores. It's a superb mountain, magnificent to look at and tremendous to look out from. Its soaring, bulky mass dominates the view up Glen Nevis, especially from the Lower Falls, and it is often mistaken for Ben Nevis. The top is capped with pale quartzite blocks, frequently erroneously thought to be snow. The beautiful scalloped little corrie just to the north of the summit is well seen from Ben Nevis.

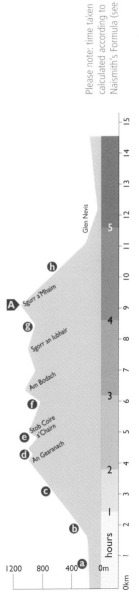

Please note: time taken calculated according to Naismith's Formula (see p.2)

The views from the top are extensive. You can look right down Glen Nevis and north to Ben Nevis, the Aonachs and the Grey Corries while to the east the long tortuous crest of the Mamores stretches out. South lie the peaks of Glen Coe. Further afield, on a clear day the Paps of Jura, Schiehallion, Ben More and Stob Binnein, Ben Lomond, Ben Lui and Ben Cruachan all stand out and many more peaks are visible.

The name means 'Peak of the Breast', presumably from the rounded shape when seen from afar. This fits in with the range as a whole as the word Mamore probably comes from mam mor or large breast.

h From the summit cairn descend north-west following the rim of the shallow northern corrie for a few hundred yards until you pick up a path. This leads steadily down the north-west ridge, zigzags down the Sron Sgurr a'Mhaim, and eventually joins the path beside the Allt Coire a'Mhusgain. This reaches Glen Nevis at the Lower Falls from where it is just over 1 mile (1.6km) of road walking up the glen to the start. It is possible to descend the north-east ridge of Sgurr a'Mhaim but this finishes with a steep descent of the steep slopes west of Steall Falls where many people have gone astray.

Sgurr a'Mhaim and the Devil's Ridge

AONACH BEAG & AONACH MOR

Aonach Mor and Aonach Beag are both over 4,000ft (1,220m) and the highest points on the 5½ mile (9km) ridge that runs between Glen Spean in the north and Glen Nevis in the south. It's a superb high level ridge, quite narrow in places, and with excellent views of Ben Nevis and Carn Mor Dearg to the west and the long, twisting line of the Grey Corries to the east. Due to the disfiguring ski resort on the northern slopes of Aonach Mor the mountains are best climbed from Glen Nevis. After a walk through the Nevis Gorge to the upper Glen steep slopes lead to the southern end of the ridge. Following the climb of the two summits a descent can be made to the col with Carn Mor Dearg and then down scenic Coire Giubhsachan back to Glen Nevis.

START/FINISH:
Glen Nevis road end. There is a summer bus service from Fort William to the Lower Falls in Glen Nevis, just over a mile (1.6km) from the road end

DISTANCE:
10 miles (16km)

APPROXIMATE TIME:
6–9 hours

HIGHEST POINT:
4,048ft (1,234m) Aonach Beag

MAPS:
Harvey's Walker's Map & Superwalker Ben Nevis, OS Outdoor Leisure 38 Ben Nevis & Glen Coe, OS Landranger 41 Ben Nevis, Fort William and surrounding area

REFRESHMENTS:
Cafes in lower Glen Nevis, all services in Fort William

ADVICE:
Some steep sections. Potential navigation problems in mist. Very serious in winter conditions

Sgurr a'Bhuic and Stob Coire Bhealaich

a The walk starts at the car park at the road end in Glen Nevis and takes the path up the wonderful wooded Nevis Gorge (see Walk 2) to the flat meadows of upper Glen Nevis.

b Continue along the path in the upper glen for just over ½ mile (1km), with views of the tremendous Steall Falls to the south, to the Steall ruins.

c From the Steall ruins there is a rough path that climbs at least halfway up the slopes towards Sgurr a'Bhuic. Leave the path at the ruins and strike north-east up rough slopes

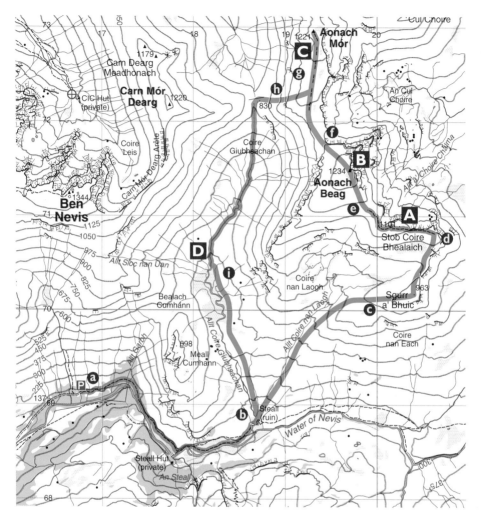

towards Coire nan Laogh (Corrie of the Calf). The quickest, but dullest, route to Aonach Beag is up the south-west ridge, on the west side of the corrie, a steep plod up featureless slopes. Longer, but recommended due to the much better views, is the climb up the right side of the corrie to the little 3,159ft (963m) pointed quartzite top of Sgurr a'Bhuic (Peak of the Buck), the southernmost summit of the Aonach ridge.

d From Sgurr a'Bhuic there are fine views east to the Grey Corries and south to the Mamores. A short stony descent leads quickly to a col at 2,915ft (885m). Beyond the col climb the slopes to the north to the rocky summit ridge of 3,611ft

(1,101m) Stob Coire Bhealaich. There are some good stretches of path leading to the summit. To the east broken cliffs mark the start of a rocky wall that stretches northwards for over 3 miles (5km).

A Stob Coire Bhealaich 202 709

This peak is a good viewpoint for Aonach Mor, whose rounded stony slopes rises to the north-west, its eastern slopes falling away dramatically in a tangle of dark buttresses, crags and scree slopes some 2,300ft (700m) to the corrie floor far below. The name means Peak of the Corrie of the Pass and it soars above the pass to the east that separates Coire Bhealaich in the north from Coire a'Bhuic in the south.

e   From Stob Coire Bhealaich the path descends a little then starts up the slopes of Aonach Beag before fading away. Continue up beside the edge of the cliffs to the summit

B Aonach Beag 196 715

At 4,048ft(1,234m) Aonach Beag is the seventh highest mountain in the Highlands. The summit cairn abuts the steep drop to the east. In winter and spring huge cornices can build up here so care should be taken not to venture out onto snow slopes east of the cairn. The summit is a fine viewpoint, especially to the west over the Carn Mor Dearg arete to massive Ben Nevis whose steep curving southern slopes drop nearly 4,000 dizzyingft (1,220m) in just over a mile (1.6km) to Glen Nevis. In contrast, the Grey Corries to the east appear quite delicate, a thin sinuous line of pale quartzite snaking into the distance.

Although the higher of the two summits, Aonach Beag means Little Ridge, while Aonach Mor means Big Ridge. The names however were given long before the Ordnance Survey came along and measured the heights of the summits and refer to the overall bulk of the mountains. In this respect Aonach Mor is clearly the much bigger hill.

f   The summit of Aonach Mor lies barely a mile (1.6km) to the north of Aonach Beag but the route between the two isn't that simple, especially in poor visibility. The convex slope leading down from Aonach Beag is steep just above the narrow col between the two mountains which is at a height of about 3,500ft (1,085m). There are crags to either side so care is needed to keep to the right line.

Please note: time taken calculated according to Naismith's Formula (see p.2)

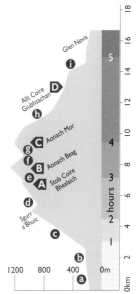

g From the col it's an easy walk up the fairly gentle slopes above to the long summit ridge of Aonach Mor. There is a reasonably well-defined path to the summit.

C   Aonach Mor   192 729

The great glory of Aonach Mor is the wild, rough and remote corries that lie on its eastern flanks. An Cul Choire in particular is a wonderful complex tangle of rock and water. The views of the Grey Corries and over Carn Mor Dearg to the great cliffs of Ben Nevis are good. The actual summit cairn is not the best viewpoint however as it is in the middle of the flat summit. The short walk to each edge is worthwhile as then the depths below can be seen with the neighbouring mountains rising above them.

The mountain itself consists of an almost level ridge over a mile (1.6km) in length. Although the walking is easy the ridge is relatively narrow and there are steep slopes to either side that can make navigation in poor visibility or when the mountain is snow-covered quite difficult. As on Aonach Beag massive cornices can build up on the eastern rim of the summit ridge. These are very impressive but also potentially very dangerous.

On the northern flanks of Aonach Mor there is an alpine ski resort complete with gondola, pylons, lifts, fencing and the other intrusive junk essential to mechanised mass skiing. An ascent aided by this machinery (gondola and chair lifts in winter, gondola alone in summer) is possible but to my mind being accompanied by developments almost to 4,000ft completely ruins the wild feel of the mountain.

h To start the descent retrace your steps from the summit down towards the col with Aonach Beag. Before the col is reached, however, turn west to descend a rough steep spur (192 722) to the bealach at 2,722ft (830m) that lies between the Aonachs and Carn Mor Dearg with the long Allt Daim glen to the north and Coire Giubhsachan to the south. There is a path down the scree-covered spur but it is very eroded and slippery. The path down the spur can be difficult to find, but there is a faint path which leads to a smallcairn at the top of the spur.

D   Allt Coire Giubhsachan   185 694

The glen of the Allt Coire Giubhsachan which runs for 2 miles (3.2km) from the bealach between Aonach Mor and Carn Mor Dearg down to Glen Nevis is very beautiful. The great high walls of Ben Nevis and the Carn Mor Dearg arete and Aonach Beag rise steeply on either side while down the centre runs the clear stream, sweeping over slabs of red and gold granite and tumbling in white cascades into pale green swirls and then slowing into deep calm pools that undercut the banks. In spring and early summer hard banks of snow often remain, bridging the water in places.

i   There isn't much of a path down Coire Giubhsachan but the walk is easy over grass and peat, though boggy in places. Once down at the Steall ruin the outward route is taken back down the Nevis Gorge to the road in Glen Nevis.

The east face of Aonach Mor

SGURR CHOINNICH MOR

START/FINISH:
Glen Nevis road end. There is a
summer bus service from Fort
William to the Lower Falls in
Glen Nevis, just over a mile
(1.6km) from the road end

DISTANCE:
11 miles (18km)

APPROXIMATE TIME:
6–9 hours

HIGHEST POINT:
3,592ft (1,095m)

MAPS:
Harvey's Walker's Map &
Superwalker Ben Nevis, OS
Outdoor Leisure 38 Ben Nevis
& Glen Coe, OS Landranger 41
Ben Nevis, Fort William and
surrounding area

REFRESHMENTS:
Cafes in lower Glen Nevis, all
services in Fort William

ADVICE:
Some steep and narrow
sections. Care needed when
under snow. Can be very boggy
in upper Glen Nevis

Although not the highest, Sgurr Choinnich Mor is arguably
the finest of the peaks on the long Grey Corries ridge. It's
a tapering, pointed peak, a long thin wedge rising above
the Water of Nevis. Although it can be linked with the rest of
the ridge to the east this makes for a long day as do any
approaches from the north as it lies far south of Glen Spean.
The easiest ascent is from Glen Nevis, an excellent walk that
leads into the bleak upper glen above Steall.

a   Leaving the car park at the end of Glen Nevis the walk begins, like Walk 19, by taking the path through the majestic Nevis Gorge past Steall Falls to the Steall ruins.

b   From the ruins there are two options. The most direct route is to climb diagonally up the slopes of Sgurr a'Bhuic to the col at 2,394ft (731m) that lies between Stob Coire Bhealaich and Sgurr Choinnich Beag. There are some steep, craggy sections of hillside south of Sgurr a'Bhuic so this is a route best left for a fine day when they can be circumvented.

c   The alternative route is to continue on the path beside the Water of Nevis for just over 1 mile (1.6km) into the boggy upper reaches of Glen Nevis. Not far past the dogleg the

Sgurr Choinnich Mor

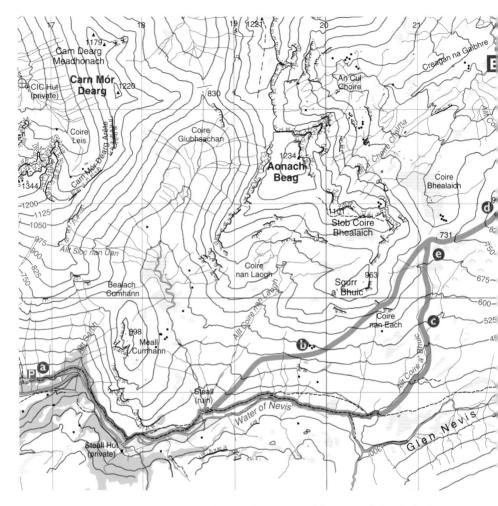

stream makes at the mouth of Coire na Gabhalach the path crosses the Allt Coire a'Bhuic. The path can be left here and the grassy slopes beside the stream climbed to the unnamed bealach. Little lochans dot the bealach which is in a fine situation below the very steep, craggy eastern slopes of Stob Coire Bhealaich.

d East of the bealach, gradually steepening and narrowing slopes lead up to the little 3,159ft (963m) grassy top of Sgurr Choinnich Beag. A short dip follows before the final climb to the summit of Sgurr Choinnich Mor at 3,589ft (1,094m).

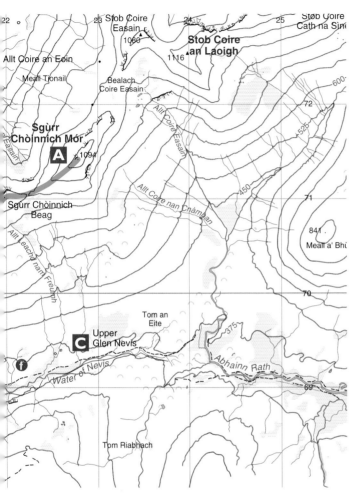

A Sgurr Choinnich Mor 227 714

Although at the western end of the Grey Corries Sgurr Choinnich Mor doesn't have the vast pale quartzite screes and blocky quartz rock ridges of the other peaks in the range. Instead it's a darker peak with grey-brown rocks and deep green grassy slopes. The mountain is cone-shaped with a neat little summit. It's possibly the best viewpoint for Aonach Beag and Aonach Mor (Walk 19) whose long massive craggy east face lies spread out to the west. There are fine views of the Mamores too, with the wedge-shaped summit of Binnein Mor looking particularly impressive as it towers over the symmetrical cone of Binnein Beag.

Please note: time taken calculated according to Naismith's Formula (see p.2)

The name means the Big Peak of the Moss, probably a reference to the boggy ground in Glen Nevis to the south.

B Allt Coire an Eoin 215 720

To the north of Sgurr Choinnich Mor lies a long, wild and interesting glen, impressive to look down into and well worthy of exploration. The burn in this glen is formed by the small streams that run down from the eastern cliffs of Aonach Mor and Aonach Beag and the north-western slopes of Sgurr Choinnich Mor. Once united these waters are known as the Allt Coire Eoin until they enter the vast plantations of Leanachan Forest after which they're called The Cour. The terrain in this glen is incredibly complex and rough with rock everywhere. If you want to venture into its depths the best access points are either from the bealach below Stob Coire Bhealaich or the bealach between Sgurr Choinnich Beag and Sgurr Choinnich Mor

e The descent can be made by either of the two ascent routes described above though the one beside the Allt Coire a'Bhuic is much the easier. Alternatively the steep but fairly

even slopes directly south of Sgurr Choinnich Mor can be descended to the Water of Nevis near the boggy head of Glen Nevis at Tom an Eite.

C Upper Glen Nevis 235 694

The head of Glen Nevis lies in a morass of peat hags and the scene is one of bleak bogs and tussocks giving way to grey and brown rough grass covered slopes, a total contrast to the rich woodlands found lower down the glen. The stream gives life to the scene, a sparkling torrent that rushes and tumbles over its stony bed. To the south soar the peaks of the Mamores and, to the west, the cliffs of Aonach Beag with the bulky half-dome of Ben Nevis beyond them. The Grey Corries aren't so impressive from here, consisting mostly of a featureless grassy slope rising above the Allt Coire Rath.

f A path, very wet in places except in long dry spells, runs down the glen beside the river to the ruins at Steall and the route through the Nevis Gorge back to the car park at the road end in the lower glen.

View east to Sgurr Choinnich Beag and Sgurr Choinnich Mor from Stob Coire Bhealaich

THE EASTERN MAMORES

🚩 🐾 🌿 🌱

START/FINISH:
Kinlochleven. There is a
Gaelicbus from Fort William

DISTANCE:
9 miles (15km) or
11 miles (18km)

APPROXIMATE TIME:
6–7 hours (short option) 8–9
hours (long option)

HIGHEST POINT:
3,706ft (1,130m) Binnein Mor

MAPS:
Harvey's Walker's Map &
Superwalker Ben Nevis, OS
Outdoor Leisure 38 Ben Nevis
& Glen Coe, OS Landranger 41
Ben Nevis, Fort William and
surrounding area

REFRESHMENTS:
Kinlochleven has cafes, chip
shops and bars

ADVICE:
Steep in places. Care required
in winter conditions

Superb high level ridge walking above deep corries and shining lochans characterises the Eastern Mamores. A network of excellent stalkers' paths provides good access from the south and gives a number of options when high in the hills. This walk includes Binnein Mor, the highest peak in the Mamores, plus the other three Munros at this end of the ridge.

a Opposite the police station on the B863 through Kinlochmore, the part of Kinlochleven that lies north of the River Leven, a signpost for the Grey Mare's Waterfall points down Kieran Road towards a small white church. The walk begins in the small car park beside the church from which a waymarked path heads up the wooded hillside. Be careful as there are many other unwaymarked trails. Alternatively, those with cars could drive up to Mamore Lodge (see Walk 4) and, for a small fee, park there and start the walk by following the track and path that runs east for just over 1 mile (1.6km) to where it meets the path from the Grey Mare's Waterfall car park.

b After a few hundred yards the path forks. The left branch heads for the Grey Mare's Waterfall, the roar of which can be heard through the trees, and then north into Coire na Ba. The walk descends by this route but for the ascent take the right fork which climbs up a spur between two stream ravines. At first the walk is through lush birch woods and deep bracken but the trees are soon left behind and the views begin to open out. The long narrow sea arm of Loch Leven stretches out to the west with the pointed peaks of Beinn na Caillich and Sgurr na Ciche rising steeply either side.

c The path reaches the landrover track from Mamore Lodge to Loch Eilde Mor after just over a mile (1.6km) and 1,280ft (390m) of ascent (GR 208 635). Cross the track and continue up the stalker's path as it angles across the hillside to the steep southern spur of Sgor Eilde Beag where it divides. There is a choice to be made here. The shorter walk takes the left branch, which zigzags steeply up the slopes above (see route description i below). The longer walk climbs more gently northwards into Coire an Lochain. I'll discuss the latter first.

d Coire an Lochain is a large corrie containing a sizeable lochan in a superb wild setting. Across the lochan 3,312ft

(1,010m) Sgurr Eilde Mor rises as a massive cone of scree, its slopes scoured with gullies. There are several ways, all steep and bouldery, up the peak. Perhaps the easiest is to take the path round the north shore of the lochan then follow a rough path that winds steeply up the rocks and scree of the west ridge and the north-west face.

A   Sgurr Eilde Mor   231658

This is the easternmost of the Mamores summits and the most remote. Cut off from the other peaks by the deep bowl of Coire an Lochain it isn't really part of the main ridge and has a feeling of isolation and separateness. There are fine views of the steep eastern flanks of Binnein Mor, which blocks the rest of the Mamores from view, adding to the feeling of this being a solitary hill. To the east though the views are vast and spacious, taking in a great expanse of much lower rounded hills that stretch out to the rolling summits around Loch Ossian. There is a clear sense of being at the end of a mountain chain. The name means Big Peak of the Hind.

Sgurr Eilde Mor from Sgor Eilde Beag

e   From the summit retrace the route back to Coire an Lochain then follow the stalkers path north down into the wild

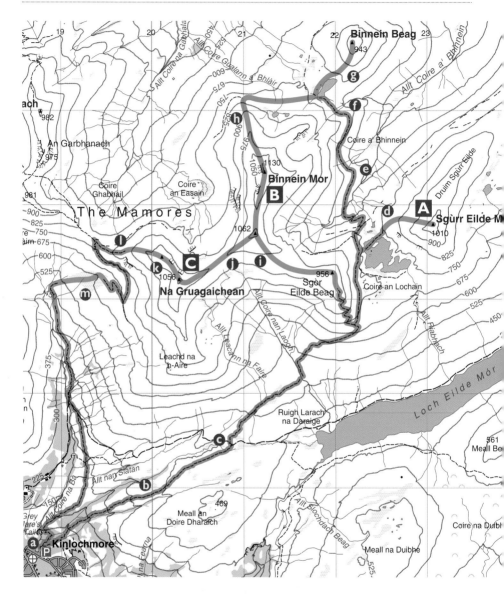

and scenic Coire a'Bhinnein below the great rocky east face of Binnein Mor.

f The well-made path is a delight as it traverses round the mountainside from the Allt Coire a'Bhinnein, rising slowly to the wide, boggy bealach at 2,460ft (750m) between Binnein Mor and Binnein Beag, where there is a small lochan.

Binnein Mor from Binnein Beag

g North-east of the bealach 3,093ft (943m) Binnein Beag (Little Peak) rises as a steep, scree-covered cone. The ascent is rough and arduous but worthwhile as the summit is a superb viewpoint for Binnein Mor. Ben Nevis looks impressive too and there are also good views of the Water of Nevis and the bleak watershed of Tom an Eite that separates Glen Nevis from the Abhainn Rath with the featureless southern slopes of the Grey Corries rising above. Descend by the same route.

h From the bealach there are two routes up Binnein Mor, whose daunting looking slopes rise directly above. The direct route is to scramble up the craggy buttress immediately above the lochan. Much easier is the gentler, grassier north-west ridge of the mountain which can be reached by contouring across the foot of the northern corrie of the peak.

B   Binnein Mor   212 663
Binnein Mor is the highest peak in the Mamores. Appropriately the name means Big Peak. Although it appears as a graceful pointed summit from some viewpoints to the north and south, it has a roof- or tent-like mien when seen from the east or west due to the short, flat summit ridge.

Binnein Mor commands a splendid view west along the rest of the range with the bulky pyramid of Sgurr a'Mhaim prominent. Across Glen Nevis towers the great curving sliced-off whaleback of Ben Nevis and the spire of Carn Mor Dearg with Aonach Beag and the Grey Corries stretching out eastwards

Please note: time taken calculated according to Naismith's Formula (see p.2)

Binnein Mor from Sgor Eilde Beag

from them. Directly to the east Sgurr Eilde Mor can be seen though this peak looks far more impressive from Binnein Mor's subsiduary southern top, confusingly called Sgurr Eilde Beag, from where it rises massive and volcano-like above the dark waters of the lochan that gives Coire an Lochain its name.

i   The two options for this walk connect on the top of Binnein Mor. To reach there via the shorter route take the zigzag path up the southern spur to Sgor Eilde Beag, from where Binnein Mor appears as a tiny pointed spire, then follow the edge of the big eastern corrie round to the South Top at 3,483ft (1,062m) and then north to the summit.

j   From the summit descend to the South Top then continue down south-west to the col below 3,464ft (1,056m) Na Gruagaichean. A short, steep climb leads to the summit.

C   Na Gruagaichean 203652
The fourth Munro in the Eastern Mamores, Na Gruagaichean lies on the main ridge between the north projecting spurs of Binnein Mor and An Gearanach and its ascent is usually combined with one or both of these, both of which can be clearly seen from the top. Oddly, though, the most impressive neighbouring peak is the mountain's own steep-sided North-west Top which lies just a few hundred yards away but is separated from the main summit by a steep 200ft (60m) drop. The name refers to both summits as it means the Maidens.

k The descent to the col and the re-ascent to the North-west Top is on very steep, rocky terrain with some big drops into Coire an Easain to the north-east. Under snow and ice this section requires great care.

l The walking is easy again beyond the North-west Top with a grassy descent west to the wide bealach between Coire Ghabhail and Coire na Ba.

m From the bealach a stalkers path descends south into Coire na Ba, traversing back and forth across the hillside in its upper reaches then following the left bank of the Allt Coire na Ba to reach the landrover track from Mamore Lodge. The path continues the other side of the track down a broad spur into rich woodlands and past the Grey Mare's Waterfall to join the start of the walk just above the car park.

View from Binnein Mor to Ben Nevis and Carn Mor Dearg rising above a sea of mist in Glen Nevis

KINLOCHLEVEN TO SPEAN BRIDGE

START/FINISH:
Kinlochleven and Spean
Bridge. There is a Gaelicbus
from Fort William to
Kinlochleven and Scotrail trains
and Highland Country buses
from Spean Bridge to Fort
William

DISTANCE:
18½ miles (30km)

APPROXIMATE TIME:
10–14 hours, can be split over
two days

HIGHEST POINT:
2,000ft (610m)

MAPS:
Harvey's Walker's Map Ben
Nevis, Harvey's Superwalker
Ben Nevis, OS Outdoor Leisure
38 Ben Nevis & Glen Coe, OS
Landranger 41 Ben Nevis, Fort
William and surrounding area

REFRESHMENTS:
Kinlochleven and Spean Bridge
have cafes, chip shops and
bars. No facilities en route

ADVICE:
Boggy in places with one river
ford that can be impassable
after heavy rain or snowmelt.
The walk goes through remote
country. There are two bothies
en route

This long through-route follows the line of an old cattle drover's track, skirting the eastern edge of the Mamores and the Grey Corries and crossing three passes in remote country. There is a feeling of spaciousness and isolation and a great sense of the vastness of the Highlands. An ascent of the remotest peak in the Grey Corries, Stob Ban, can be made.

a   Like Walks 4 and 21 the walk begins in the Grey Mare's Waterfall car park in Kinlochleven from where a waymarked path heads up the wooded hillside. To reach the car park take the B863 road through Kinlochmore, the part of Kinlochleven that lies north of the River Leven, to where a signpost for the Grey Mare's Waterfall points down Kieran Road towards a small white church. The car park is next to the church.

View over Loch Eilde Mor to the distant Aonach Eagach

b   After a few hundred yards the path forks. The left branch heads for the Grey Mare's Waterfall, the roar of which can be heard through the trees. The short diversion to see the falls is worth making. From the junction take the right fork, which climbs up a spur between two stream ravines. At first the walk is through lush birch woods and deep bracken but the trees are soon left behind and the views begin to open out

with the long narrow sea arm of Loch Leven stretching out to the west with the pointed peaks of Beinn na Caillich and Sgurr na Ciche rising steeply either side.

View west up the Abhainn Rath to the Mamores and a cloud shrouded Ben Nevis

c   The path reaches the landrover track from Mamore Lodge to Loch Eilde Mor after just over a mile (1.6km) and 1,280ft (390m) of ascent (GR 208 635).

d   Turn right on the landrover track and follow it to Lochs Eilde Mor and Eilde Beag.

A   Loch Eilde Mor   218 636

This long loch, along with smaller Loch Eilde Beag, lies in the defile that separates the Abhainn Rath glen from Loch Leven. The low watershed is just beyond the lochs so the waters from both drain south into the River Leven though some of it is drawn off down a big pipeline that contours round the hillside to feed the Blackwater Reservoir (see Walk 8).

The immediate surroundings of the lochs are fairly featureless with the steep, even slopes of the eastern Mamores rising to the north and lower rounded boggy hills rolling away to the south and east. However there is an excellent view south-west to the distant serrated ridge of the Aonach Eagach (see Walk

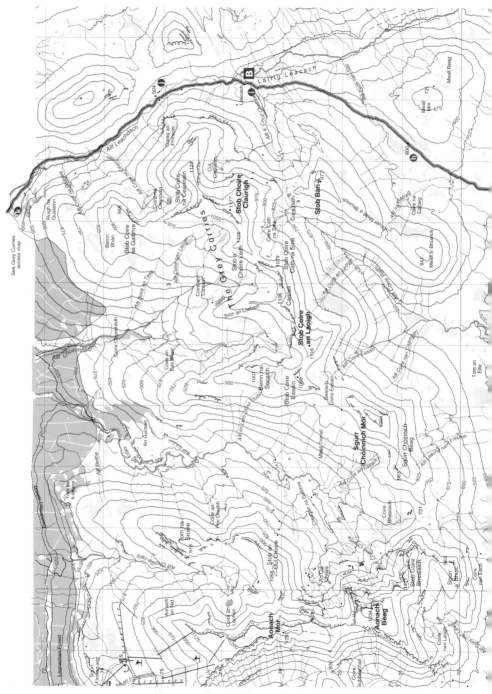

Please note: 1km = 1.625cm on this map

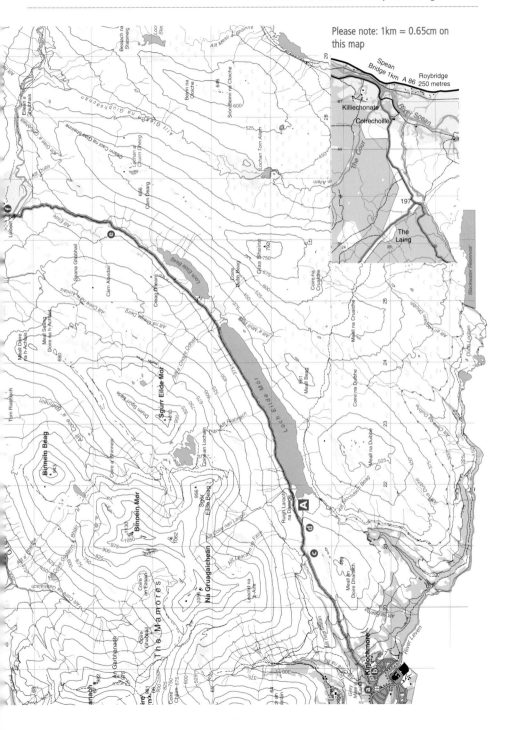

Please note: 1km = 0.65cm on this map

29) from the green sward at the western end of Loch Eilde Mor. The name means the Big Loch of the Hind and there is a good chance of seeing deer on the slopes round about.

e From Loch Eilde Beag the track rises very gently to the indistinct watershed with the hills to the north slowly appearing then gradually descends to the ruined house at Luibeilt and the Abhainn Rath.

f Crossing the Abhainn Rath is the only potentially difficult and dangerous part of the walk. Much of the time the water is no more than ankle deep and the ford is easy. When the river is in spate however it can be a roaring torrent that is completely impassable. In such conditions you have to either retrace your steps to Kinlochleven or else head upstream seeking a safer crossing place. If one isn't found continue on over Tom an Eite to the Water of Nevis and follow this stream down to the road in Glen Nevis and Fort William.

g Once across the river take the path north beside the Allt nam Fang. Just to the east there is a bothy, Meanach, maintained by the Mountain Bothies Association (see Fact File) that could be used as a shelter in case of bad weather.

h The path climbs through featureless terrain to a wide boggy pass between the bump of Meall Mor and Stob Ban, an outlier of the Grey Corries and a fine peak though it doesn't look it from this side. The pass, at 2,000ft (610m), is the highpoint of the walk.

i From the pass the path angles down across the lower slopes of Stob Ban into the Lairig Leacach, arriving in the glen at the Lairig Leacach bothy.

Lairig Leacach bothy and Sgurr Innse

B   Lairig Leacach 282 736

Whilst useful as an emergency shelter the bothy is tiny and can't sleep more than a few people so you shouldn't plan on using it for an overnight shelter. The situation is impressive with steep mountain walls rising up on either side. To the east lie the twin Munros of Stob Coire Easain and Stob a'Choire Mheadhoin with to the north of them two rugged Corbetts, Sgurr Innse and Cruach Innse. The first of these, 2,683ft (818m) Sgurr Innse, is a very fine rugged, fortress-like mountain that is well worth the scramble to the summit. To the west there is an excellent view up the Allt a'Chuil Choirean to Stob Ban, from here an impressive soaring pointed peak rising steeply above the narrow wooded gorge. There is a great contrast between the dark confines of the ravine and the pale quartzite pyramid of the peak – the name means White Peak – which shines in bright sunlight. Stob Ban, the lowest Munro in the Grey Corries at 3,204ft (977m) is a very remote peak lying south of the main Grey Corries ridge and with over a thousandft (305m) of re-ascent back to the ridge if climbed with the other peaks. The Lairig Leacach makes a good start point for an ascent and there should be time to climb the peak if this walk is being done over two days. There is a rough path up the north-east ridge. You can return by descending very steep boulders and scree to the bealach to the north, where there is a small tarn, and then down a huge staircase of quartzite slabs to the Allt a'Chuil Choirean.

j   From the bothy a broad track climbs very slowly up to the top of the Lairig Leacach at 1,653ft (504m) and then descends beside the Allt Leachdach with the steep eastern rim of the Grey Corries rising above.

k   A few hundred yards after the track crosses the Allt Leachdach on a small bridge it enters the vast conifer plantations of the Leanachan Forest. After ½ mile (800m) or so in the trees the track crosses the line of an old narrow gauge railway, built to assist with construction of the tunnel taking water from Loch Treig to the east under the mountains to the aluminium works in Fort William. Skirting the forest now, the track continues for another mile down to the farm of Corriechoille and a minor road that runs for 2½ miles (4km) along the south side of the River Spean to Spean Bridge. The road isn't busy and makes a pleasant finish to the walk as fine deciduous woods line each side and there are good views of the rushing river.

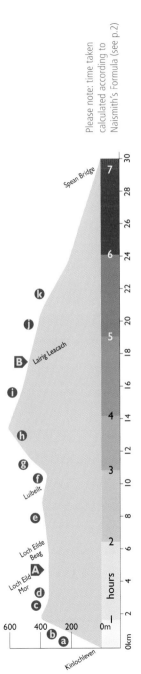

BEINN A'BHEITHIR & GLEANN AN FHIODH

START/FINISH:
Information Centre,
Ballachulish. Gaelicbus from
Fort William

DISTANCE:
10 miles (16km)

APPROXIMATE TIME:
5–7 hours

HIGHEST POINT:
3,361ft (1,024m) Sgorr Dhearg

MAPS:
OS Landranger 41 Ben Nevis,
Fort William and surrounding
area

REFRESHMENTS:
Cafes and bars in Ballachulish

ADVICE:
Steep sections, no path in
places

A steep climb and a fine high level walk over three summits with superb views of mountains and sea lochs followed by a steep descent to a wild glen. Beinn a'Bheithir is a magnificent horseshoe-shaped mountain that towers over the narrows of Loch Leven and the Ballachulish bridge. However much of the northern side has been sullied by grim ranks of conifer plantations. Finding a way through these can be difficult and frustrating so this route climbs Beinn a'Bheithir from the east then descends southwards to return along scenic Gleann an Fhiodh.

A Ballachulish Tourist Information Centre 083 583

Ballachulish is an old slate mining village with a growing number of attractions for visitors. There is a large car park outside the Information Centre. As well as the usual tourist material the Centre has an interesting display on the slate industry.

a   From the car park walk past the information centre, cross the road ahead and continue south-west past a supermarket and some playing fields. Follow this road for 550 yards (0.5km) to where it turns west and crosses the river Laroch. Immediately across the bridge turn left up a minor road, signposted 'Public Footpath to Glen Creran', that climbs past a church and the primary school and out of the village. (This is the same start as Walk 11).

Beinn a'Bheithir is pronounced Ben Vare. Most books give the meaning as Hill of the Thunderbolt but according to Peter Drummond in his *Scottish Hill and Mountain Names* this is only one of many possibilities. He says the mountain is named for the Celtic goddess of winter and death. Beithir means a baleful demon and the mountain was said to be the home of a female demon, the Cailleach Bheithir, who caused floods but who sometimes appeared as a beautiful woman. Drummond says *bheithir* can also mean a bear or a serpent.

Beinn a'Bheithir and Loch Leven

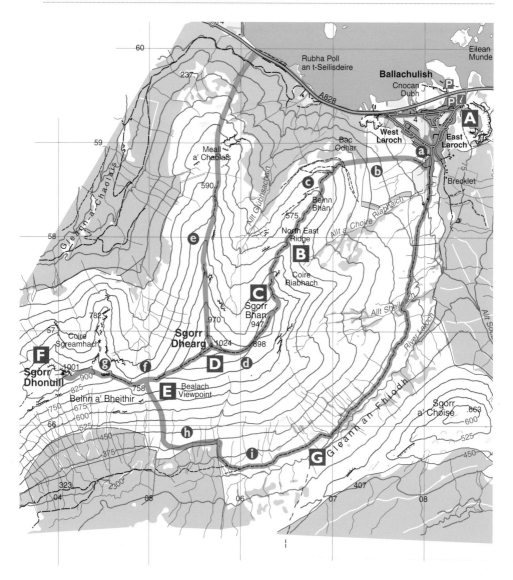

b Immediately past the primary school take the first gate on the right. There is a fence to cross at about 500ft (150m). Continue to climb the hillside above, on grass at first and then heather, to reach a broad ridge.

c On the ridge a path runs southwards to the first summit, Sgor Bhan (3,104ft/947m), which isn't named on the OS Landranger map.

B The North East Ridge of Sgorr Bhan 069 565

As you climb the easy north ridge to Sgorr Bhan the slanting ledges of dark slate that make up the precipitous face of the north-east ridge can be seen to the left. There is an easy scrambling route up this ridge.

C Sgorr Bhan 063 561

From Sgorr Bhan a beautifully elegant narrow arete curves round to Sgorr Dhearg. This graceful arcing ridge looks particularly attractive when snow covered.

d A rough path leads from Sgorr Bhan to Sgorr Dhearg, whose neat summit is topped by the broken stump of a triangulation pillar.

D Sgorr Dhearg 056 558

The whole of the summit ridge of Beinn a'Bheithir gives superb views. Sgorr Dhearg is the highest point and a good place to stop and enjoy the surrounding panorama. Mountains dominate the scene to the north and east with the peaks of Glen Coe, the Mamores and the great bulk of Ben Nevis all prominent. South-westwards Loch Linnhe stretches out into the distance to the Firth of Lorn with the hills of Ardgour and Morvern beyond it and further south Ben More on Mull and the distinct cones of the Paps of Jura. To the west the summit ridge of Beinn a'Bheithir dips down to a col then climbs to the dark granite dome of Sgorr Dhonuill. The rock on Sgorr Dhearg is a pink quartzite – hence the name, which means red peak.

e Alternative route. A cairn just beyond the summit of Sgorr Dhearg marks the top of the north ridge, which can be followed down to the forest and the A828 road about twokm from Ballachulish if you want to shorten the walk. Be warned though that there can be difficulties finding a way through the trees.

f To continue the main walk descend from Sgorr Dhearg by the broad stony ridge that runs west-south-west to a bealach crossed by a broken down wire fence at 2,450ft (757m). To the north lies conifer clad Gleann a'Chaolais, into which a descent can be easily made though the plantation has then to be negotiated. Southwards lies the watershed between Glen Duror and Gleann an Fhiodh. This is also wooded but the trees cease just over the divide in Gleann an Fhiodh. This is the way back to Ballachulish so a choice has to be made here, either to go up Sgorr Dhonuill first (see g) or else descend from here.

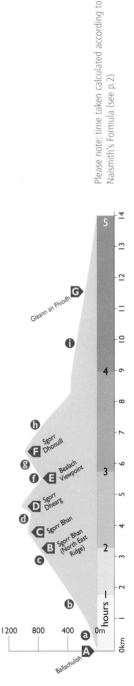

Please note: time taken calculated according to Naismith's Formula (see p.2)

Ballachulish means the town of the narrows. The two ends of the village are known as East and West Laroch. There is a legend that Fingal, a great Celtic hero, defeated the Vikings here and that their King, Erragon, and his followers were buried at Laroch. The site is now itself buried under debris from the slate quarries.

E   Bealach Viewpoint 048 555

At the bealach there are good views ahead to the rugged slopes of Sgorr Dhonuill (3,284ft/1,001m) and the winding, narrow east ridge. To the north of this crest dark granite cliffs and rough stony slopes fall steeply into the corrie that separates the two peaks. To the south of the bealach the rugged slopes of Fraochaidh (2,875ft/879m) rise above the plantations in Glen Duror.

g   Above the bealach an 800ft (245m) climb leads up steep, rocky slopes to Sgorr Dhonuill. There is a path through the rocks. Just below the final summit pyramid the angle eases for a short distance before a last steep but easy scramble up a narrow boulder covered ridge right on the edge of the crags to the north.

F   Sgorr Dhonuill 040 555

Although the lower of the two main summits of Beinn a'Bheithir Sgorr Dhonuill is the better viewpoint, especially to the west as there are no higher hills in that direction. The name means Donald's Peak, presumably a reference to the Clan Donald who ruled the West Highlands for many years and some of whose descendants were the MacDonald clan who were massacred in Glen Coe in 1692.

h   After taking in the views from the summit retrace your steps back down to the bealach. Steep slopes lead south towards the dense conifers at the head of Glen Duror. There is no path but the line of the fence can be followed down into the glen. Cutting across the slopes in a south-easterly direction towards the end of the plantation is possible, but there are many small crags, steep-sided knolls and, lower down, greasy slabs to be bypassed. Once the deer fence is reached the edge of the trees can be followed over rough tussocky ground to the end of the forest in upper Gleann an Fhiodh. Just to the south, near the infant River Laroch, there is a good track, the old route from Ballachulish to Glen Duror.

i   The track runs down Gleann an Fhiodh, at first close to the river and then high on the slopes above the left bank, before descending to Ballachulish.

G   Gleann an Fhiodh   078 560

Gleann an Fhiodh means Wooded Glen but, as in so many Highland glens, most of the natural woodland has long gone. This is sheep country and these animals, which close-crop the vegetation, ensure that any seedlings don't survive. However there are some small stands of birches scattered about in places while along the steep, rocky edges of the little streams that split the slopes on either side of the glen birches and rowans grow, out of reach of browsing sheep and deer.

Sgor Bhan from Sgor a'Choise

THE SUMMITS & RIDGES OF BIDEAN NAM BIAN

START/FINISH:
Achnambeithach, Glen Coe. The Citylink/Skye-Ways Glasgow to Skye and Edinburgh to Skye buses go through Glen Coe and may let passengers off near the head of the glen. Gaelicbus runs services from Fort William to Glencoe village

DISTANCE:
8½–10 miles (14–17km)

APPROXIMATE TIME:
6–9 hours

HIGHEST POINT:
3,766ft (1,150m) Bidean nam Bian

MAPS:
Harvey's Walker's Map Glen Coe, Harvey's Superwalker Glen Coe, OS Outdoor Leisure 38 Ben Nevis & Glen Coe, OS Landranger 41 Ben Nevis, Fort William and surrounding area

REFRESHMENTS:
Glen Coe NTS Visitor Centre, Clachaig Inn and Glencoe village

ADVICE:
Steep, rocky, complex terrain requiring good navigation skills. Some easy scrambling. Hazardous in winter

Bidean nam Bian is a magnificent mountain, one of the finest in the Highlands. Rather than a single peak it's a marvellously complex massif with long rugged spurs jutting out from the rollercoaster of the main ridge and pointed summits rising above cliff-rimmed deep corries. Everywhere is steep and rocky and the walking is serious and committing. This walk takes in the main summits and is a good introduction to a mountain that takes many visits to know at all well.

A The Three Sisters of Glen Coe 183 564

The summit of Bidean nam Bian is set well back from Glen Coe and is quite hard to see from the glen floor. The dominant features of the mountain are three steep-sided rocky ridges that terminate abruptly in huge dark cliffs, the famous Three Sisters of Glen Coe. The best viewpoint for these glacially truncated spurs is The Study on the hillside north of the A82 near the east end of the glen (GR 183 564). The Study is a large flat-topped rock, the name being a corruption of the Scots word for an anvil, stiddie, itself a translation of the original Gaelic Innean a'Cheathaich, Anvil of the Mist.

Gearr Aonach and Aonach Dubh from the lower slopes of Beinn Fhada

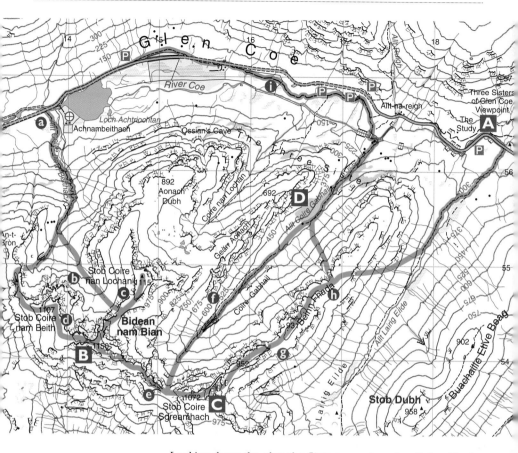

Looking down the glen the Sisters are, in order, Beinn Fhada (the long mountain), Gearr Aonach (the short ridge) and Aonach Dubh (the dark ridge). The first and last are bulky and blunt in contrast to the thin, almost elegant lines of Gearr Aonach. Rising above the Sisters is the tapering pyramid of Stob Coire nan Lochan, frequently thought to be Bidean though the actual summit is hidden from view.

a   The walk starts where the A82 road crosses the River Coe just below attractive Loch Achtriochtan. At the west end of the bridge a wooden gate marks the start. The nearby whitewashed farmhouse of Achnambeithach was where mountain rescue in Glen Coe began and is still a mountain rescue post. A path heads up beside the west bank of the Allt Coire nam Beithach (stream of the corrie of the birches) between the dark walls of the great west face of Aonach Dubh, a major rock climbing venue, and the only slightly less

Stob Coire nam Beith and Loch Achtriochtan

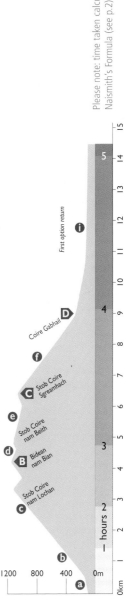

Please note: time taken calculated according to Naismith's Formula (see p.2)

First option return

Coire Gabhail **D**

f

Stob Coire
Sgreamhach **C**

Stob Coire
nam Beith **e**

Bidean
nam Bian **d** **B**

Stob Coire
nam Lochan **C**

b

a

1200   800   400   0m

rugged slopes of An-t-Sron. The path quickly steepens and there is a slight scramble before it passes above the fine waterfall issuing from the mouth of the corrie. Once badly eroded this path is now a fine example of the path builder's craft. The steepest sections have been cobbled with tightly

Stob Coire Sgreamhach and
Beinn Fhada from the Aonach
Eagach

packed stones to make a hard-wearing surface that in my view
is far preferable and less visually obtrusive than the previous
wide eroded scar.

b   Once in spectacular Coire nam Beithach, a tremendous
bowl of rock and scree backed by impressive cliffs, there are
two ways to reach the ridges above. Firstly you can head right
(west) and ascend steep scree to the low point on the ridge
between An-t-Sron and Stob Coire nam Beith. An even better
route is to turn left and follow the rough path across the
jumbled boulders and scree of the corrie floor towards the
two huge rock buttresses that wall the small upper corrie.
These are known to rock climbers as the Diamond and Church
Door Buttresses. To the left of the cliffs a path winds up the
steep scree to the col between Stob Coire nan Lochan and
Bidean itself. The path at this point is badly eroded and quite
difficult to follow. Take care.

c   From the col it's worth going out and back to the summit
of 3,657ft (1,115m) Stob Coire nan Lochan (Peak of the
Corrie of the Lochan) before making the final, steep, rocky
climb to the summit of 3,766ft (1,150m) Bidean nam Bian.

B   Bidean nam Bian 143 542
Surprisingly for such a big mountain, the summit of Bidean
nam Bian is small, a neat little pointed top perched at the

apex of three ridges. Unsurprisingly it's a superb viewpoint. Magnificent rugged hills lie on every side. To the north the serrated crest of the Aonach Eagach seems rather subdued due to its lower height. Beyond it Ben Nevis rises, big and bulky, with the rippling line of the Mamores running out east of it. Further east lies a series of long mountain ridges: nearby Beinn Fhada, beyond it the Buchailles, Etive Dearg and Etive Mor, then the Blackmount hills and further away still yet more hills fading into the distant horizon. Turning south Loch Etive stands out with Ben Starav and Ben Cruachan rising above it. Westwards Beinn a'Bheithir floats above Lochs Linnhe and Leven.

The name Bidean nam Bian is usually taken to be a corruption of Bidean nam Beann, meaning the Peak of the Hills or Mountain of Mountains, an appropriate name for a summit at the heart of such a large massif. Bidean is also the highest mountain in the county of Argyll.

d The summit of 3,631ft (1,107m) Stob Coire nam Beith (the Peak of the Corrie of the Birches) lies a little under ½ mile (800m) north-west of Bidean nam Bian. The walk there and back is quite easy and worthwhile for the precipitous view straight down into Coire nam Beith.

e The main walk descends stony slopes south-east to the col at the head of Coire Gabhail, just below the outlying summit of 3,516ft (1,072m) Stob Coire Sgreamhach. A steep rocky walk leads to the top.

C Stob Coire Sgreamhach 154 536

Stob Coire Sgreamhach is the second Munro in the Bidean massif, though it was only promoted to that status in the 1997 revision of the Tables. It's a fine peak with excellent views back to Bidean. The dramatic sounding name has an equally dramatic meaning, the Peak of the Dreadful Corrie, a reference, presumably to Coire Gabhail, which lies directly north of the peak.

f There are two options for the return to Glen Coe from Stob Coire Sgreamhach. The quickest and easiest is to return to the col at the head of Coire Gabhail, descend the steep slopes into the corrie and then follow the path down the flat floor of the corrie to the steep descent through a ravine to the road in Glen Coe.

g The second option is to head north-east to Beinn Fhada. This route is steep and rocky and involves some scrambling. After an initial steep descent the ridge runs out to a very steep nose above the col with Beinn Fhada. Confident scramblers can pick a way down this. Others will want to descend to the right (east) and find a way along a series of narrow grass and scree ledges to the col. Not far above lies the 3,116ft (952m) summit of Beinn Fhada.

h Beinn Fhada lives up to its name of Long Mountain as the walking continues, easily now, over a series of rough tops. The north-west side of the mountain is uniformly steep and craggy but south of the last top there is a gentle dip in the ridge from which a steep descent can be made down a faint path in a shallow gully to the floor of Coire Gabhail. Alternatively, though longer, a descent can be made east to the Allt Lairig Eilde and the path beside that burn (see Walk 13) followed down to Glen Coe.

D   Coire Gabhail 165 555

Coire Gabhail is very impressive. The long flat shingle floor of the corrie is the bed of an old lake, whose waters long ago broke through the narrow barrier, created by a huge landslide down Gearr Aonach, holding them in place. The entrance is now a tangle of huge boulders and trees, below which the stream drops away steeply in a narrow steep-sided gorge. A path threads its way down this impressive ravine to come out at a bridge over the River Coe beyond which lies the A82 road.

Because it is hidden from view by the narrow gorge, Coire Gabhail is often called the Lost Valley though the name actually means the Corrie of Booty, a reference to the MacDonald clan's habit of hiding stolen cattle in its depths.

i   The old road can be followed back down Glen Coe for most of the 2 mile (3.2km) walk back to the start. Only for the last ½ mile (800m) or so is it necessary to walk along the verges of the busy and fast A82. Throughout the scenery is magnificent.

Bidean nam Bian from the
Aonach Eagach

BUACHAILLE ETIVE MOR

START/FINISH:
Altnafeadh on the A82. The Citylink/Skye-Ways Glasgow to Skye and Edinburgh to Skye buses go through Glen Coe and may let passengers off at Altnafeadh

DISTANCE:
8½ miles (14km)

APPROXIMATE TIME:
6–9 hours

HIGHEST POINT:
3,349ft (1,022m)
Stob Dearg

MAPS:
Harvey's Walker's Map Glen Coe & Harvey's Superwalker Glen Coe, OS Outdoor Leisure 38 Ben Nevis & Glen Coe, OS Landranger 41 Ben Nevis, Fort William and surrounding area

REFRESHMENTS:
Kingshouse Hotel. Various establishments in Lower Glen Coe

ADVICE:
Steep, loose, rocky terrain. Difficult in mist and hazardous in winter conditions. Take care on descents in wet weather

O ne of the great mountains of the Highlands, Buachaille Etive Mor is also one of the best known as the huge rock pyramid of Stob Dearg, the highest summit, rises up from the flat wastes of Rannoch Moor in full view of northbound motorists on the A82. There is more to Buachaille Etive Mor than can be seen from the road however and this walk traverses the splendid ridge that runs south-west from Stob Dearg for 2½ miles (4km) over three more summits.

a   The walk starts at Altnafeadh on the A82 east of Glen Coe (GR 222 563). There is room for parking here. A track heads

south to a bridge over the River Coupall after which it
becomes a good, well-maintained path that heads past the
white cottage of Lagangarbh, a Scottish Mountaineering Club
hut, straight towards the daunting and seemingly impregnable
north face of Stob Dearg, an impressive and complex tangle of
rock features. However on the west side of the cliffs lies Coire
na Tulaich, which, although steep and full of boulders and
scree, gives walkers a way through to the summit ridge.
Where the path splits not far beyond Lagangarbh take the
right fork; the left branch leads to the base of the cliffs.

b   Once the boggy moor beyond the river is crossed the path
begins to climb and soon enters the rocky mouth of the corrie.
The scenery is wild and rugged and there's no doubt that this
is a big, serious mountain. The going becomes more arduous
as the path winds its way upwards over scree and boulders on

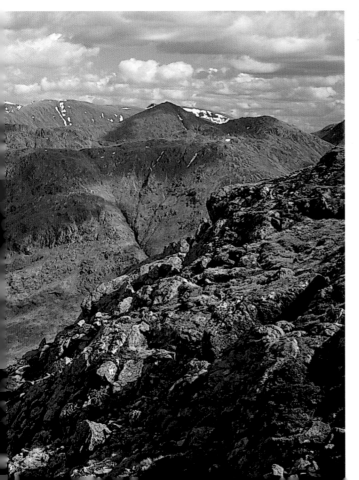

Buachaille Etive Mor from the
Aonach Eagach

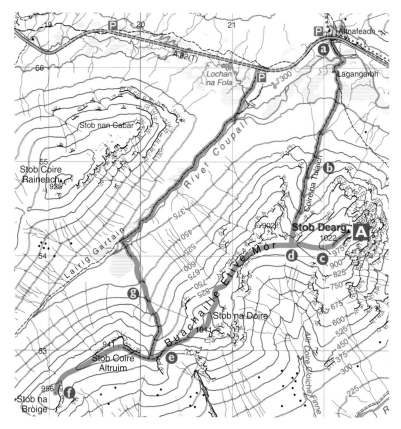

the right-hand side of the corrie to finally arrive at a narrow gully that leads steeply up to the main ridge. The path avoids this loose trench to follow the series of rocky ledges to the right to emerge on a broad stony bealach at 2,886ft (880m). The ledges are covered with loose stones and scree and there is a risk of being hit by dislodged rock here so it's wise to watch out for people above you and try not to get directly below them. Also note that in winter big cornices can build up on the lip of the corrie, making it a much more challenging route.

b From the bealach climb eastwards up boulder covered slopes to the 3,349ft (1,021m) summit of Stob Dearg. Many cairns mark the well-worn route.

A Stob Dearg 222542
Stob Dearg's large summit cairn sits right on the edge of the great east face and there is a strong sense of open space and

The east face of Stob Dearg, Buachaille Etive Mor

precipitous drops. It's a superb viewpoint for Rannoch Moor, whose flat lochan-dotted expanse stretches out to the east to distant hills. On clear days the sharp point of Schiehallion stands out beyond the moor.

Looking south-west the undulating ridge of the mountain can be seen running out to the final summit, Stob na Broige. This is the peak that dominates the view up Glen Etive along with its counterpart on Buachaille Etive Beag, Stob Dubh.

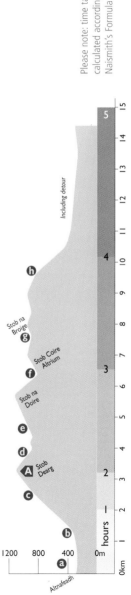

Please note: time taken calculated according to Naismith's Formula (see p.2)

Including detour

Stob na Broige

Stob Coire Altrium

Stob na Doire

Stob Dearg

Altnafeadh

Stob Dearg means Red Peak, a reference to the red-coloured igneous rock called rhyolite that makes up the cliffs and screes. Rhyolite forms great unbroken buttresses and pillars split by deep rocky gullies that make for excellent rock climbing and Stob Dearg has been one of the premier climbing destinations in the Highlands since 1894 when the great Scottish mountaineer Norman Collie made the first climbs here. Evocative names have been given to the many features of the complex north and east faces of the mountain, names such as Rannoch Wall, Crowberry Tower, Crowberry Gully, Crowberry Ridge, The Chasm, Great Gully, Slime Wall and many more, all famous in the annals of Scottish mountaineering.

Buchaille Etive More translates as the Great Herdsman of Etive, the Little Herdsman being Buchaille Etive Beag. Certainly, from lower Glen Etive the southern most tops of each mountain dominate the view to the north, a pair of matched cones rising above the forested glen floor.

c From the summit, return to the bealach at the head of Coire an Tulaich. South of the bealach lies grassy Coire Cloiche Finne (Corrie of the White Stone) which makes for an easy if steep descent to Glen Etive. Indeed, in winter if the cornices above Coire an Tulaich are big this is the best way down, as it is in poor visibility if you aren't sure of the way down into Coire an Tulaich. It's been descended inadvertently too by people who've lost their way in the mist on the featureless terrain of the bealach.

d Just above the bealach there's a minor bump followed by a gentle descent and then an ascent to 3,316ft (1,011m) Stob na Doire (Peak of the Copse) beyond which there's another drop to the lowest point on the ridge at 2600ft (810m). A short way up the next slope a rough path leaves the ridge and descends into Coire Altruim to the north and then on down to the Lairig Gartain. This is the best descent route from the ridge on the Glen Coe side. Take care on the descent in wet weather.

e Above the low point the ridge curves north of west as it climbs to the third summit, 3,080ft (939m) Stob Coire Altruim (Peak of the Corrie of the Rearing or Nursing – presumably of deer calves).

f From the summit the stony ridge continues south-west again, down to another small dip and then up to the final summit, 3,136ft (956m) Stob na Broige (Peak of the Shoe).

This summit was elevated to Munro status in the revision of the list in 1997. There is a superb view down Glen Etive to Loch Etive, as you would expect from a peak that looks so dramatic from the floor of the glen. Descents can be made down the long south-west ridge into Glen Etive or, steeply, north-west to the top of the Lairig Gartain. However the first route leaves you a long way down Glen Etive, fine if you're carrying camping gear or have arranged a lift but leaving a long walk back over the Lairig Gartain to Altnafeadh otherwise. The second route is really only worth doing if you're continuing up Buachaille Etive Beag as it's a rough stony descent. The quickest and recommended way back to Altnafeadh is to return to the col beyond Stob Coire Altruim and descend from there (see d above).

Stob Dearg, Buachaille Etive Mor

g The descent from the col is steep and stony at first then grassy and boggy. In little over ½ mile (800m) 1,475ft (450m) of height is lost. Once down cross the infant River Coupall to the good if muddy path that runs down the Lairig Gartain for just over a mile (1.6km) to the A82 (see Walk 13). Altnafeadh is less than ½ mile (800m) to the east.

THE NORTHERN BLACKMOUNT

START/FINISH:
Alltchaorunn, Upper Glen Etive

DISTANCE:
10 miles (16km)

APPROXIMATE TIME:
7–9 hours

HIGHEST POINT:
3,634ft (1,108m) Meall a'Bhuiridh

MAPS:
Harvey's Walker's Map & Superwalker Glen Coe

REFRESHMENTS:
Kingshouse Hotel

ADVICE:
Some steep terrain. Difficult in mist. Only possible in dry conditions as the River Etive has to be forded twice

Between Upper Glen Etive and Rannoch Moor lie the hills encircling huge Coire Ba known as the Blackmount. This walk ascends the two main summits in the Northern Blackmount, Creise and Meall a'Bhuiridh, plus a fine subsidiary peak, Clach Leathad, and a Corbett with an excellent view of the South Glen Coe peaks, Beinn Mhic Chasgaig. There is a superb view of the Northern Blackmount from the Glen Etive road just past the junction with the A82. As well as the tops, the route explores an exciting wild glen, that of the Allt Ghuibhasan.

a   The farm of Alltchaorunn (GR 196 510) lies on the south side of the River Etive where the Allt a'Chaorainn ('Stream of the Rowan') comes down a deep defile. Beinn Mhic Chasgaig is prominent to the east, a soaring cone of a hill. Follow the fence around the farm until you reach a broad bridge. However the far side of this bridge is barred by a locked gate topped with barbed wire so it cannot be used as a way across the river. Instead, the river has to be forded. This can be done fairly easy not far above the bridge when the water is low. In spate though the river is too dangerous to cross and another walk should be chosen for the day. Note too that the river has to be forded at the end of the day so if it turns wet cutting the walk short is a good idea.

The Blackmount (right) and Buachaille Etive Mor from the south

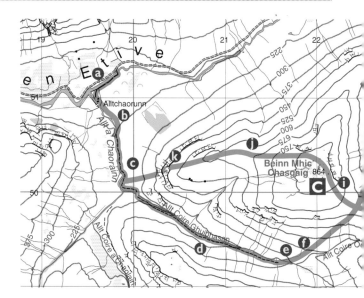

b   Once across the river a track leads to Alltchaorunn from where a path heads up the east (true right) bank of the Allt a'Chaorainn. There are some deep dark pools in the granite bed of the burn that look good for swimming in on a hot day. Birches and rowans cling to the steep sides of the burn as the ravine steepens and narrows as steep spurs from Beinn Mhic Chasgaig and, to the west, Beinn Ceitlein push down on either side.

c   After ½ mile (800m) the burn divides. The path continues up the left fork, the Allt Coire Ghuibhasan. It remains on the east bank for a 109 yards (100m) or so then descends dramatically beside a cliff along a narrow rock ledge with a wire rope as a handhold to a single plank bridge that makes for an exciting crossing of the dark confines of the gorge.

d   The path continues up the narrow, steep-sided ravine high on the slopes above the tumbling burn. Birches, alders and rowans line the slopes. In atmosphere and appearance this gorge compares with those of Glen Nevis and Coire Gabhail though it is far less well known.

e   At a height of 1,230ft (375m), just below another junction of burns, the stream makes a sharp right-angled turn and tumbles down an amphitheatre of rock in a fine waterfall. Hemmed in by high mountains this is a magical spot, redolent of all that is most wild and beautiful in the Highlands.

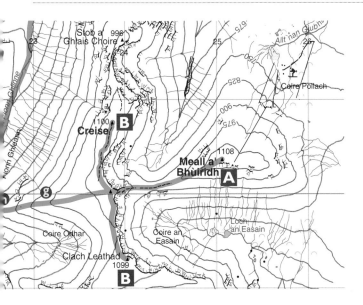

Please note: time taken calculated according to Naismith's Formula (see p.2)

f Above the waterfall the glen opens out and the burns run over granite slabs. The left fork, the Allt Coire Odhair, can be followed a short way then the rough slopes to the north climbed to the 2,312ft (705m) bealach between Beinn Mhic Chasgaig and Creise.

g Turning east an easy climb leads up a wide ridge to a 3,510ft (1,070me) minor top called Mam Coire Easain on the Creise ridge. Although insignificant in itself this is the hub for three summits with Meall a'Bhuiridh to the east, Creise to the north and Clach Leathad to the south. The last two are easy ascents on gentle grassy ground. Meall a'Bhuiridh is a bit more arduous as it involves the descent of a steep and fairly narrow rock rib to a small col and then an ascent of the rough, rocky west ridge to the summit. From the col the Allt Cam Gleann runs away northwards in a deep ravine while to the south little Loch Coire Easain glitters in its eponymous corrie. It's a fine situation.

A   Meall a'Bhuiridh 250 503

At 3,634ft (1,108m) Meall a'Bhuiridh is the highest summit in the Blackmount. The name means 'Hill of the Roaring', a reference to the wild bellowing of rutting red deer stags that can be heard echoing through the hills every autumn. 'Meall' usually means a rounded hill and often, according to Peter Drummond (*Scottish Hill and Mountain Names*), a hill amongst mountains as Mealls are usually lower than

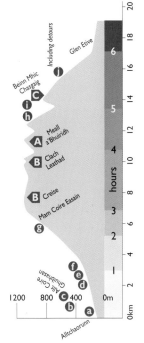

surrounding summits. This is a misnomer here as Meall a'Bhuiridh is a fine rocky peak as well as being higher than any nearby top. The name Blackmount for the whole range is a literal translation of the Gaelic Am Monadh Dubh.

There are good views across Rannoch Moor and back across the Cam Ghleann to the steep-sided, flat-topped ridge of Creise with, more impressive though lower, the more pointed peak of Clach Leathad to the south. Only a short distance from the summit however is the top of a ski tow, part of the White Corries ski resort that dominates the northern slopes of the mountain. This resort is a good reason for climbing Meall a'Bhuiridh from the west and returning the same way. There's nothing like the machinery and scarring of a ski area to destroy the wildness and beauty of the mountains.

B   Creise 238 506 & Clach Leathad 240 493
The summit of Creise is the highest point on the long ridge that runs south north for some 2½ miles (4km) from the Bealach Fuar-chataidh that divides it from the Southern Blackmount hills to the rocky spur of Sron na Creise that rises above the boggy ground at the mouth of Glen Etive. At 3,608ft (1,100m) Creise is slightly lower than Meall a'Bhuiridh but it's clearly the dominant mountain of the massif with Meall a'Bhuiridh simply the, admittedly high, end of a side spur. From Creise Meall a'Bhuiridh appears as a symmetrical red rock pyramid.

Clach Leathad used to be the Munro on the ridge until remeasurement in the early 1980s showed Creise to be the higher peak.

The meaning of Creise is unknown, the name being so corrupted that its derivation cannot be traced. Clach Leathad means the Stone of the Slope.

h   Once the three main summits have been climbed the west ridge of Mam Coire Easain can be descended back to the bealach below Beinn Mhic Chasgaig. If another ascent doesn't appeal you can either retrace the route into Coire Ghiubhasan or descend straight, boggy Fionn Ghleann (White Glen) to the north into Glen Etive.

j   From the bealach it's an easy 522ft (159m) climb to the flat summit of 2,834ft (864m) summit of Beinn Mhic Chasgaig.

C   Beinn Mhic Chasgaig 221 502

The flat summit plateau of Beinn Mhic Chasgaig can be a confusing place in mist. The small cairn marking the highest point lies at the north end. There is a good view west across the deep trench of Glen Etive to Buachaille Etive Mor with Bidean nam Bian beyond it.

Beinn Mhic Chasgaig is MacChasgaig's Hill though who MacChasgaig was is long forgotten.

k   The steep west ridge of Beinn Mhic Chasgaig can be descended back to Alltchaorunn but this is a difficult descent. An easier way down is by the long north ridge, which gives good views of Buachaille Etive Mor, though this leaves a walk of almost 2 miles (3km) down Glen Etive to the start.

Waterfall on the Allt Coire Ghuibhasan

STOB COIR'AN ALBANNAICH & MEALL NAN EUN

START/FINISH:
Lower Glen Etive. Postbus (Monday to Saturday) to Glen Etive Post Office from Fort William and Glencoe

DISTANCE:
10½ miles (17km)

APPROXIMATE TIME:
6–8 hours

HIGHEST POINT:
3,425ft (1,044m) Stob Coir'an Albannaich

MAPS:
Harvey's Walker's Map & Superwalker Glen Coe, OS Landranger 50 Glen Orchy and surrounding area

REFRESHMENTS:
None in Glen Etive. The Kingshouse Hotel is just off the A82 near the head of Glen Etive

ADVICE:
Some steep terrain. Navigation in mist can be difficult. Care is required in winter conditions

Stob Coir'an Albannaich is a massive wedge of a hill running from Lower Glen Etive to Upper Glen Kinglass. Connected to it by a neck of high ground containing a minor top is Meall nan Eun, a much smaller, very steep-sided hill. There are good views from both summits. Linking the two hills gives a circular walk through two scenic glens, those of the Allt Mheuran and Allt Ceitlin, with a finish along the lush banks of the River Etive.

a To reach Glen Etive turn off the A82 at the signposted junction opposite the road that leads to the Kingshouse Hotel. There are a number of small parking places beside the road in the lower glen. The walk itself starts where a track leaves the road (GR 131 464) and runs down to the river. From here to the Robber's Waterfall (GR 139 450) the route followed is the same as for Walk 6 where a more detailed description will be found.

b Follow the path along the river bank to a small gorge with rocky wooded walls where a footbridge crosses the river.

C There are two ways up Stob Coir'an Albannaich. The most

Stob Coir'an Albannaich

direct, but also the most arduous and least scenic (though there are good views of Ben Starav), is to head directly up the slopes above to the minor top of Beinn Chaorach (hill of the sheep) and then along the broad north-west shoulder over flat slabs of granite to the summit.

d Alternatively turn right at the fork in the track just beyond the bridge, soon passing the house at Coileitir. Just past the house the path divides again. This time take the left fork, which climbs across some boggy ground through open birch woodland to the Allt Mheuran.

e The path now follows the east (true right) bank of the Allt

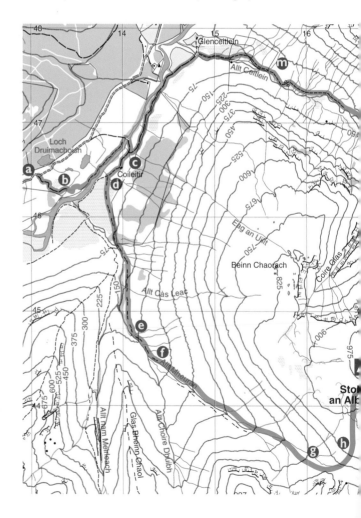

Mheuran past the Eas nam Meirleach or Robber's Waterfall, an impressive double drop into a dark gorge. There are excellent views across Glen Etive to massive Bidein nam Bian (see Walk 24). Above the waterfall there are some attractive waterslides.

f   The stream divides not far above the waterfall. Keep left here on the now muddy and, in places, hard to follow path as the glen opens out. The steep-sided dome of Glas Bheinn Mhor (see Walk 28) is prominent to the south.

g   The path crosses the stream and continues up the far side to the bealach at 2,411ft (735m) between Glas Bheinn Mor

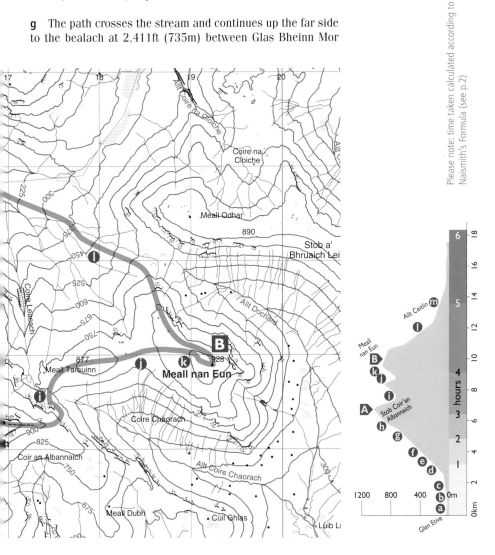

Please note: time taken calculated according to Naismith's Formula (see p.2)

The summit of Stob Coir'an Albannaich with Glas Bheinn Mhor and Ben Starav in the background

and Stob Coir'an Albannaich. On the far side you can look down into upper Glen Kinglass.

h From the bealach climb north-east up initially steep slopes to the south-east spur (called Sron nan Cabar by the OS but unnamed on the Harvey maps) of Stob Coir'an Albannaich then continue up much gentler grassy slopes to the summit. If descending this way in mist take care to leave the spur at the right point as it's easy to follow it too far down into Glen Kinglass.

A   Stob Coir'an Albannaich 169 443

Stob Coir'an Albannaich stretches over 5 miles (8km) from north-west to south-east, a massive hill with mostly smooth rounded slopes on the west but complex, steep, rocky terrain to the east. The 3,425ft (1,044m) summit is marked by a large well-built cairn with a smaller one on top of it set right on the edge of the north-east face. The views of the Glen Coe and Blackmount hills are extensive without being spectacular.

Glas Bheinn Mhor and Ben Starav from Stob Coir'an Albannaich

The name means Peak of the Corrie of the Scotsmen, the actual corrie of this name lying south-east of the summit, its mouth guarded by a deep narrow gorge. The name is taken to refer to the first Scots immigrants from Ireland.

i   The continuation of the walk to Meall nan Eun involves some complex route-finding which can be difficult in poor visibility. Good compass skills are required. Steep crags abut

Stob Coir'an Albannaich from Meall nan Eun

View down the glen of Allt
Ceitlin to Glen Etive

the summit so initially it is necessary to descend a steep rib
in an easterly direction. This soon turns to the south-east.
Before it does so, after barely 550 yards (0.5km), a more level
section is reached. Here turn sharply just west of north and
drop steeply through craggy ground to the lochan dotted col
below 2,877ft (877m) Meall Tarsuinn.

j   Tarsuinn means cross over or transverse and it's usually
applied to hills that go against the grain of the land. This
Meall Tarsuinn is no exception as it runs east-west while the
bigger hills to either side lie north-west to south-east. Meall
Tarsuinns also often lie between higher hills and have to be
climbed or skirted en route. In my experience it's usually
easier to go over the top. Traversing steep hillsides can take
a surprisingly large amount of time and effort.

k   On the far side of Meall Tarsuinn fairly gentle slopes lead
to the north-west ridge of Meall nan Eun up which it is an
easy walk to the summit.

B Meall nan Eun 192 449

3,044ft (928m) Meall nan Eun is an extremely steep-sided but flat-topped hill. Only the north-west ridge gives a gentle ascent. The name means Hill of the Birds.

l To descend return north-west across the plateau and continue on down the hillside in the same direction. To the west the long, ragged, rocky east face of Stob Coir'an Albannaich, the mountain's most impressive feature, dominates the view. Just before the Allt Ceitlin is reached two deep, rocky, birch-clad ravines, Coire Leacach and Coire Glas, with a steep spur between them, can be seen cutting through the crags. In places there are extensive granite pavements which make for good walking, a relief from the otherwise somewhat boggy and tussocky terrain.

m Once the mass of burns seaming the hillside come together to form the Allt Ceitlin and the steep walls of Stob Dubh and Beinn Chaorach close in on either side cross to the right side of the burn where a path leads down to the farm of Glenceitlin and Glen Etive. A track leads south beside the river to the bridge at Coileitr and so back to the start.

Stob Coir'an Albannaich (left) and Glas Bheinn Mhor

BEN STARAV & GLAS BHEINN MHOR

START/FINISH:
Lower Glen Etive. Postbus
(Monday to Saturday) to Glen
Etive Post Office from Fort
William and Glencoe

DISTANCE:
10 miles (16km)

APPROXIMATE TIME:
6–8 hours

HIGHEST POINT:
3,536ft (1,078m) Ben Starav

MAPS:
Harvey's Walker's Map &
Superwalker Glen Coe, OS
Landranger 50 Glen Orchy and
surrounding area

REFRESHMENTS:
None in Glen Etive. The
Kingshouse Hotel just beyond
the head of Glen Etive is the
nearest place for refreshments

ADVICE:
Some steep terrain. Navigation
in mist can be difficult. Care is
required in winter conditions

Ben Starav is a magnificent mountain, rising steeply and abruptly from Loch Etive in a great rocky pyramid seamed and riven by stream gullies. It looks particularly majestic from the slopes of Beinn Trilleachan on the far side of the loch. This walk climbs Ben Starav by its long north ridge then follows a rugged crest to Glas Bheinn Mhor before descending the scenic glen of the Allt Mheuran.

a The start is the same as for Walks 6 and 27 at the track in lower Glen Nevis, at GR 131 464, that runs down to the river from the road. A path is then followed along the riverbank to a small gorge with rocky wooded walls where a footbridge crosses the river.

b Turn right at the fork in the track just beyond the bridge, soon passing the house at Coileitir. Just past the house the path divides again. Stay right, beside the River Etive, and follow the path across boggy ground to the Allt Mheuran, here attractively lined with trees – Scots pine, birch, holly, rowan. Just upstream there is a bridge. On the far side the path

Ben Starav and Loch Etive from Beinn Trilleachan

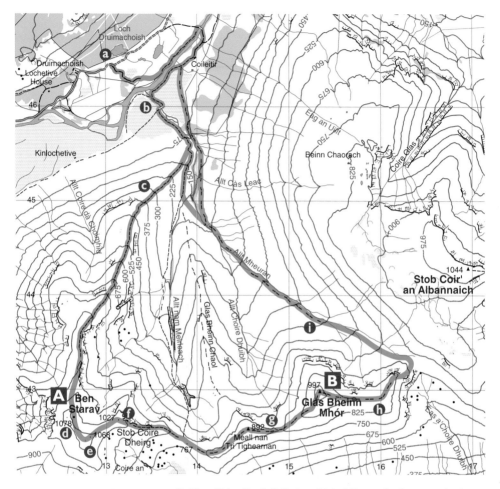

divides. Take the left fork, which follows the burn to the base of the north ridge of Ben Starav.

c The north ridge rises in one great sweep of over 3,280ft (1,000m) to the 3,536ft (1,078m) summit of Ben Starav, making it a satisfying if arduous ascent route. The angle is unrelenting except for two short shoulders at around 1,640ft and 2,625ft (500 and 800m). Apart from a short section where another ridge merges with it at 2,625ft (800m) the ridge is well defined with steep slopes falling away on either side. There are great views across to the steep dome of Glas Bheinn Mor. Near the top the ridge, rocky now, steepens and narrows and runs along the edge of some small crags.

View up the Allt Mheuran to Glas Bheinn Mhor

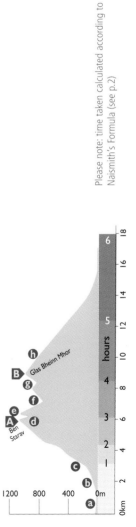

Please note: time taken calculated according to Naismith's Formula (see p.2)

A Ben Starav 125 427

The summit of Ben Starav is a superlative viewpoint and it's worth walking to each edge to get the best of the views. Perhaps the most stunning vista is to the west where extremely steep slopes fall dizzyingly right down to sea level and shining Loch Etive, beyond which rises Beinn Trilleachan with the Trilleachan Slabs glistening on its flanks. Following the line of Loch Etive south leads the eye to a fine view of the twin summits of Ben Cruachan. In really clear weather the distant Paps of Jura can be seen just to the right of Cruachan. Turning south through east to north to north-west reveals a mass of hills from Ben Lui and the Bridge of Orchy summits to the Blackmount and the Glen Coe peaks.

The meaning of Ben Starav is unclear and there are various possibilities. Drummond (*Scottish Hill and Mountain Names*) says it could be from *starbhanach*, a well-built person, or *starra*, a block of rock, but settles for *starabhan* as the most likely as this means a rustling noise which he takes as referring to deer as in the case of Meall a'Bhuiridh, the Hill of Roaring, which lies not far away. The 1997 edition of *Munro's*

Tables agrees, translating it as hill of rustling though with a qualifying maybe. However Peter Hodgkiss gives it as 'stout hill with small head' in the SMC *District Guide to the Central Highlands* while Irvine Butterfield has 'strong mountain' in *The High Mountains of Britain and Ireland* and Ralph Storer 'Bold Mountain' in his *100 Best Routes on Scottish Mountains* though he does qualify this with a possibly. Perhaps the best course is to play safe like the SMC *Hillwalkers' Guide to The Munros* which simply says 'origin unknown'.

d   Care is required when descending from Ben Starav in poor visibility as the ridge twists and turns and there are cliffs and steep slopes to the north and east. Initially the way is south-east for a few hundred yards to a slight rise at 3,503ft

Glas Bheinn Mhor and Ben Starav

(1,068m). Two ridges lead away from this bump. One heads north-east to the 3,372ft (1,028m) subsidiary top of Stob Coire Dheirg (Peak of the Red Corrie), the other goes south to two more subsidiary tops, 3,050ft (930m) Meall Cruidh (Hill of the Hardness) and 3,011ft (918m) Stob an Duine Ruaidh (Peak of the Red-haired Man).

e Unless you are climbing all the Tops the north-east ridge is the one to follow. This takes the form of a narrow rock arete with some easy scrambling, though most of this can be avoided to the south. There is a good view back to the main summit from Stob Coire Dheirg.

f Continue on down the narrow east ridge of Stob Coire Dheirg. There are rows of huge pinnacles and rock turrets just to the left. In misty conditions these look like huge teeth as they loom out of the swirling clouds. The descent is steep and stony but not difficult. The top of the ridge can be hard to locate in poor visibility however and there is a danger of descending north-east along a short spur that ends in a sheer drop. To ensure the right ridge is located go south initially from the top of Stob Coire Dheirg for 55 yards (50m) or so and then turn east.

g The ridge ends at a col at 2,516ft (767m) below the minor bump of 2,926ft (892m) Meall nan Tri Tigheaman, whose name translates as the grandiose sounding Hill of the Three Lords. Beyond this top lies the west ridge of 3,270ft (997m) Glas Bheinn Mhor.

B Glas Bheinn Mhor 153 429
The mossy summit of Glas Bheinn Mhor – Big Grey-Green Hill – is an excellent viewpoint for Ben Starav and across Glen Etive to the hills south of Glen Coe.

h Steep broken crags prevent descent northwards to the Allt Mheuran so the main ridge should be followed east from the summit. This ridge starts with a short descent then levels off before turning north-eastwards after 765 yards (700m). It then steepens abruptly immediately above the bealach at the head of the Allt Mheuran. These final slopes are rough and craggy but an easy enough way can be found down, keeping right to avoid the crags.

i From the bealach descend the glen of the Allt Mheuran, picking up a path on the left side of the burn. Just before the Allt Choire Dhuibh the path crosses to the right bank and

continues down beside the now attractively wooded gorge. The fine Robber's Waterfall is passed and then the path divides. Either fork leads to the River Etive but the right one is the quickest way back to Coileitir, the bridge over the River Etive and so to the start.

Stob Coire Dheirg and Glas Bheinn Mhor from Ben Starav

THE AONACH EAGACH

START/FINISH:
Allt-na-reigh, Glen Coe. The Citylink/Skye-Ways Glasgow to Skye and Edinburgh to Skye buses go through Glen Coe and may let passengers off in the glen. Unless transport can be arranged it's necessary to walk back up Glen Coe to the start from the finish by Loch Achtriochan

DISTANCE:
8 miles (13km)

APPROXIMATE TIME:
4–6 hours

HIGHEST POINT:
3,172ft (967m) Sgorr nam Fiannaidh

MAPS:
Harvey's Walker's Map & Superwalker Glen Coe, OS Outdoor Leisure 38 Ben Nevis & Glen Coe, OS Landranger 41 Ben Nevis, Fort William and surrounding area

REFRESHMENTS:
Glen Coe NTS Visitor Centre, Clachaig Inn and Glencoe village

ADVICE:
Steep exposed terrain. Good scrambling skills and a head for heights required. A serious mountaineering venture in winter

The Aonach Eagach is the most exciting and spectacular ridge walk on the Scottish mainland, a rollercoaster of rock pinnacles, buttresses, gullies and slabs. It's not difficult but a good head for heights is needed if the traverse is to be enjoyable rather than terrifying. There are good views from the ridge but it's the immediate surroundings that make this walk worthwhile rather than distant panoramas. It's a committing scramble as there are no descent routes into Glen Coe between Meall Dearg at the east end of the ridge and Stob Coire Leith near the west end. There are two Munros and two subsidiary Tops on the ridge. Other than the descent route from Ben Nevis, this is the most popular route described in this book and large numbers can be expected on dry sunny summer days.

a   The easiest way to walk the Aonach Eagach is generally reckoned to be from east to west and that is the direction described here. At the very least it involves 500ft (150m) less ascent as it starts from higher up in Glen Coe. The climb to the ridge is also more interesting this way though no less arduous. The start is just west of the buildings of Allt-na-reigh where a signposted path leaves a small car park and heads steeply up the shoulder of Am Bodach (the Old Man) towards

Sgorr nam Fiannaidh

The Aonach Eagach rising above Glen Coe

the Allt Ruigh. The last means the 'stream of the outstretched base of a mountain', i.e. a ridge. *Ruigh* is Gaelic for forearm and the name comes from the similarity of the landform to this limb.

b The path mostly stays beside the Allt Ruigh until the burn fades away not far below the ridge crest though it does make one big zigzag out onto the shoulder of Am Bodach to avoid a steep gorge. There are excellent views from this shoulder back across Glen Coe to Bidean nam Bian and down the glen to Loch Achtriochtan.

c The steep path emerges from the confines of the Allt Ruigh glen onto the col between the bump of Sron Garbh and Am Bodach. The 3,093ft (943m) summit of the latter is a short but steep and rough walk to the west.

d The scrambling starts on the descent from Am Bodach. The ridge leaves the summit heading just north of west. Not far below the summit cairn some very steep outward sloping polished rock ledges with a sheer drop below them have to be descended. These are particularly unnerving when wet as they are then very slippery. When under snow and ice this is the hardest part of the traverse. Beyond this descent – the one section of the ridge that is definitely easier in the other direction – the going is a little easier as a path winds along the narrow rocky ridge crest to Meall Dearg.

A Meall Dearg 161 583
3,126ft (953m) Meall Dearg is one of the two Munros on the Aonach Eagach. It has a place in the history of Scottish

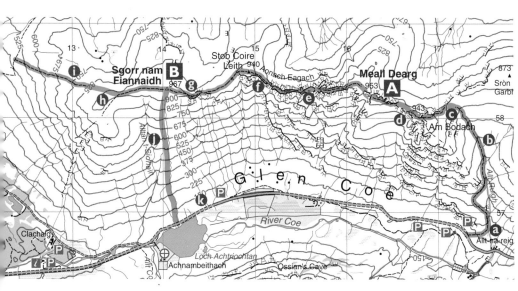

mountaineering as the final summit climbed by the Rev. A.E.Robertson in his first ever round of all the Munros. Robertson climbed Meall Dearg in 1901 and is famous (or infamous) for kissing the cairn before his wife. Curiously, he didn't do the actual Aonach Eagach, climbing the two Munros separately.

The name means Red Hill after the pinkish rock of the crags and screes. Meall usually denotes a rounded lump, an inapt description here.

e The Aonach Eagach proper runs between Meall Dearg and Stob Coire Leith. The name means Notched Ridge and that's an accurate description. From Meall Dearg the ridge is a twisting, turning narrow rock arete replete with jagged turrets and steep rock steps. Depending on how you feel about clambering over big rocks above big drops, the spectacular view along the ridge from Meall Dearg is either exciting or terrifying. None of the scrambling is difficult however and on a dry sunny day the traverse is a delight, the rough volcanic rock warm to the touch, giving a confidence that is often lacking in wind and rain. In places paths cut below the ridge, avoiding some of the scrambling. Often though these paths are more exposed and hazardous than the route along the ridge crest as there are no secure handholds. The hardest section – known as the Crazy Pinnacles – comes near the end. The ridge is at its narrowest here and the contorted pinnacles hang over the drops, hence the name. Beyond them is a steep

View east along the Aonach Eagach

drop down a polished slab to a narrow neck of ground with a very steep climb out the other side. This is felt by many to be the hardest part of the traverse, especially when heading west to east.

f After the Crazy Pinnacles and the negotiation of the gap, the last few rocky turrets are easily negotiated. Beyond them the ridge broadens to give a simple walk up to 3,083ft (940m) Stob Coire Leith (Peak of the Grey Corrie). Old iron fence posts mark the way. From the summit you can look back along the ridge with a feeling of satisfaction at successfully completing the traverse.

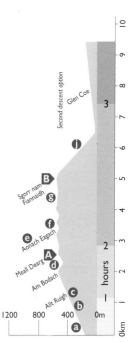

Please note: time taken calculated according to Naismith's Formula (see p.2)

View west along the Aonach Eagach to Stob Coire Leith and Sgorr nam Fiannaidh

g A pleasant ridge walk leads on to the last peak, 3,172ft (967m) Sgorr nam Fiannaidh. For much of this last section the rock is white quartzite in contrast to the dark volcanic rocks of the pinnacles.

B   Sgorr nam Fiannaidh 140 583

Although the highest peak on the Aonach Eagach, Sgorr nam Fiannaidh feels isolated from the real rocky heart of the ridge as this is now some distance away and partly hidden by the intervening summit of Stob Coire Leith. Sgorr nam Fiannaidh is an excellent viewpoint however, with a superb view right up Coire nam Beithach to Bidean nam Bian on the far side of Glen Coe and an equally excellent one down Loch Leven and over the Ballachulish Bridge to the steep pyramid of Garbh Bheinn in Ardgour on the far side of Loch Linnhe.

The name means Peak of the Fian Warriors, a reference to the story that the great Celtic mythical hero Fingal and his followers fought a battle with the Vikings on the lower flanks of the mountain (see Walk 12 for more details).

h There are two good descent routes from Sgorr nam Fiannaidh and one poor, not to say dangerous, one. The latter is the worn-out, appallingly loose and eroded scar of scree and boulders– path is too good a description – that runs from the summit down the extremely steep hillside on the west side of the long impressive chasm of the Clachaig Gully to reach the glen not far from the Clachaig Inn. This route is right next to sheer drops into the gully in places and there have been several accidents so it is definitely not a good way down.

i The easiest descent is to continue west from Sgorr nam Fiannaidh to a subsidiary top then descend north-westwards a short distance and pick up a path that angles down the hillside to join the path that climbs to the col with Sgorr na Ciche (see Walk 12). This path then leads easily if boggily down to the old road in the glen. The problem with this route if you don't have a vehicle at this end is that it's a long 4¼ mile (7 km) walk back up the glen to the start. You can stop at the Clachaig Inn for refreshment en route of course.

j The way down that leaves the shortest distance up the glen to the start is the direct descent from the summit to Loch Achtriochtan. This descent is rough and unrelentingly hard on the knees as the hillside drops very steeply for almost 3,000ft (915m) without a break but there are no problems as long as you don't stray west towards the gully of the Alltan-t-Sidheir. There are bits of a path but they are hard to find and to follow.

k Once down in the glen it's a little under 2 miles (3km) back to the start. Much of this can be walked on the old road.

The Aonach Eagach seen over Meall Mor from Sgorr a'Choise

BEN NEVIS VIA THE CARN MOR DEARG ARETE

START/FINISH:
Glen Nevis Visitor Centre.
Highland Country bus from
Fort William – journey time ten
minutes

DISTANCE:
10 miles (16km)

APPROXIMATE TIME:
8–10 hours

HIGHEST POINT:
4,406ft (1,344m)
Ben Nevis

MAPS:
Harvey's Walker's Map &
Superwalker Ben Nevis, OS
Outdoor Leisure 38 Ben Nevis
& Glen Coe, OS Landranger 41
Ben Nevis, Fort William and
surrounding area

REFRESHMENTS:
Cafes & bars in Glen Nevis

ADVICE:
Rough, stony terrain. Some
steep sections with easy
scrambling. Navigation can be
very difficult in poor visibility.
To be avoided when snow-
covered except by experienced
mountaineers

This long, steep walk up Britain's highest mountain is one of the best hill walks in Britain. The route is rough and stony and there is some scrambling involved. A good head for heights is needed for the Carn Mor Dearg arete. In winter this is a serious mountaineering expedition. The scenery, especially the views of Ben Nevis' finest feature, the massive cliffs of the north face, is magnificent.

A   Glen Nevis Visitor Centre 124 731
The Visitor Centre has much interesting information on Ben Nevis and Glen Nevis and is well worth a visit.

a   From the visitor centre cross the bridge over the River Nevis, turn right and follow a signposted path which leads to the track that starts at Achintee Farm. There is also roadside parking opposite the youth hostel in Glen Nevis (GR 128 718), from here cross the bridge over the River Nevis and follow the path straight up the steep hillside opposite.

b   The path joins another path rising diagonally from the left across the slopes of Meall an t-Suidhe. Turn right and take this path, which is the main route up the mountain. There are

Ben Nevis and Carn Mor Dearg
from the Mamores

a couple of steep zigzags then the path climbs in a steep curve above the Red Burn before easing off as the saddle holding Lochan Meall an t-Suidhe is reached.

Ben Nevis from upper Glen Nevis

B   Pony Track 133 722

The track rising diagonally across the slopes of Meall an t-Suidhe from the left follows the line of the old Pony Track, built in Victorian times at a cost of £800. At first it served the observatory which was open from 1883 to 1904. Part of the observatory was later opened as a hotel, which operated until 1918. During this period charges were made for using the track. The Pony track is the easiest way up Ben Nevis but also the least scenic and better used for the descent. It is often called the Tourist Track but this is a misnomer as it is a serious route that takes the walker into increasingly wild and dangerous terrain. There have been many accidents, some of them fatal, on this path. Lochaber Mountain Rescue Team, who bring down those who get into difficulties, would like the route to be renamed the Mountain Track.

C   Lochan Meall an t-Suidhe 144 725

A rather desolate sheet of water lies in a boggy saddle between Ben Nevis and the outlying bump of Meall an t-Suidhe. The Gaelic name means the 'lake of the hill of the seat', after the hill that rises directly above it to the west, but

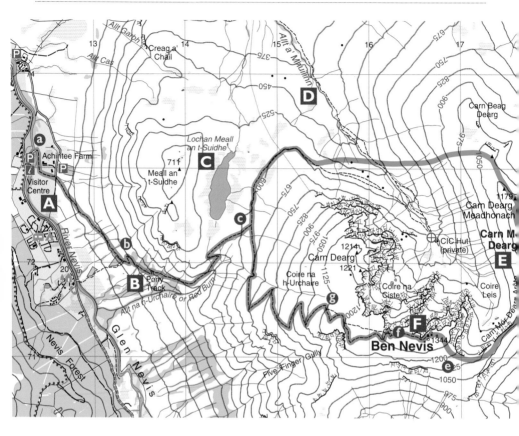

it is sometimes called the Halfway Lochan though it lies at only 1,850ft (550m).

c Continue on the path as it crosses the saddle and climbs the lower slopes of Ben Nevis to a junction. Here the main track turns sharply right while our route contours across the slopes to the left. After rounding the north-west shoulder of Carn Dearg the path enters the Allt a'Mhuillin glen. Leave the path here and descend to the stream (note that there is no more water on the walk until near the end so fill your bottles here), cross it, and climb up the heather covered slopes on the far side to the small bump of Carn Beag Dearg. Now follow the stony ridge over Carn Dearg Meadhonach to Carn Mor Dearg.

D   Allt a'Mhuillin 159 733
This glen is in the heart of spectacular scenery. As you enter it you can see ahead reddish stony slopes leading to the long ridge and the tiny pointed summit of Carn Mor Dearg. Once

The North Face of Ben Nevis from the slopes of Carn Mor Dearg

down at the stream you can look up to the vast cliffs of Ben Nevis. Two miles (3km) long and reaching 2,000ft (610m) in height, they are the biggest in Britain. The name is a common one in the Highlands as it means Stream of the Mill and many streams were used to power mills. Another Allt a'Mhuillin is found on the slopes of Sgorr na Ciche (see Walk 12).

E Carn Mor Dearg 177 722
The tiny summit of Carn Mor Dearg is a magnificent viewpoint for the north face of Ben Nevis. Across the Allt a'Mhuillin lie deep corries, soaring rock aretes and gigantic cliffs, famous worldwide for the superb rock and ice climbing. The tiny building by the stream is the Charles Inglis Clark (C.I.C) Hut, built in 1929 by the Scottish Mountaineering Club and used as a base by climbers. To the east of the summit a steep, narrow ridge falls away to a col, the watershed between the Allt Daim and the Allt Coire Giubhsachan, beyond which rise the long steep western flanks of Aonach Mor and Aonach Beag. The name Carn Mor Dearg means big red cairn, from the pink granite screes on its slopes. (Carn Dearg Meadhonach means middle red cairn and Carn Beag Dearg little red cairn).

d From the summit of Carn Mor Dearg a graceful narrow rocky arete curves symmetrically round the head of Coire Leis to the boulder covered slopes leading to the summit of Ben Nevis. The scramble along the arete is quite easy but the situation is wild and this is a glorious place to be. The views of the cliffs are superb throughout. The rough blocks of granite give good grip and the few exposed places can be easily circumvented on faint traversing paths.

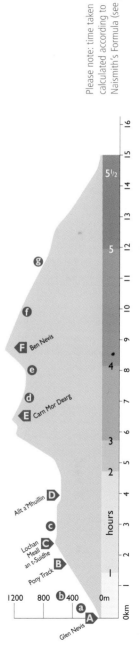

The Allt a'Mhuillin and the cliffs of Carn Dearg

The first person known to have climbed Ben Nevis was a botanist called James Robertson who made the ascent in 1771 to collect plants for Edinburgh University. However in the nineteenth century it became popular with tourists. In 1881 Clement Wragge of Fort William first collected weather data for the Scottish Meteorological Society, climbing to the top every day during the summer, a feat he repeated the following year.

The first recorded tourist ascent took place in 1787. The party had three guides and four soldiers to act as porters. The venture took thirteen hours.

In 1895 the first Ben Nevis Race was held. It still takes place on the first Saturday in September. The record for the ascent and descent of the Tourist Track is an amazing 1 hour and 45 minutes. Most walkers take well over six hours.

e   The low point before the final ascent is just 3,478ft (1,060m) so there is still quite a climb to the summit of the Ben. The thin line of the arete ends at the base of a massive boulder slope. On the right here a line of three abseil posts for use by winter climbers lead down into Coire Leis. Although there are occasional cairns, a few metal posts and bits of path, there's no clear track up the chaos of steep boulders. The important thing to remember is that there are cliffs to the right so you need to keep well out in the middle of the boulder field. The summit arrives suddenly as the slope eases off. A cluster of cairns appears and then the triangulation point can be seen on top of a large, well-built cairn. Nearby lie the remnants of the observatory with a small emergency shelter perched on top. There are far too many cairns and memorials scattered over the summit area often along with piles of litter. Please don't add to these.

F Ben Nevis 166 713

The views from the summit are spacious but curiously uninspiring. Everything seems so small and far away! The best views are in fact from the edge of the cliffs and in clear weather it is worth walking over to the rim and following it a short way while you peer down the massive buttresses and deep gullies, perhaps seeing some rock climbers spread-eagled on the sheer cliffs.

The meaning of Nevis is unclear. The most popular idea is that it derives from either 'nimheil' or 'nibheis', Gaelic words meaning evil or venomous. Given the prevailing wet and windy weather conditions these would be appropriate names.

f The way off Ben Nevis is by the main Mountain Track. However descending from the summit plateau requires care as the path passes very close to the edge of the cliffs. A line

Carn Mor Dearg and the Carn Mor Dearg Arete

The North Face of Ben Nevis from the upper slopes of Carn Mor Dearg

of large cairns marks the route across the plateau to the start of the main path. In thick mist and especially if the ground is snow-covered and the path hidden careful compass work is needed to keep to the right line. From the trig point walk 500ft (150m) on a bearing of 231° to avoid the cliffs then continue down on a bearing of 281°, being careful not to stray left (south-west) into Five Finger Gully, a notorious spot for accidents. In 1996 some marker posts were erected at the head of Five Finger Gully by the Lochaber Mountain Rescue Team to assist with navigation in difficult conditions. These have proved very controversial with many mountaineers opposing their presence. Whether they will stay is open to question. It is, anyway, unwise to rely on artificial markers.

Ben Nevis from the east

g   The Mountain Track leaves the summit plateau and heads down the mountain in a series of long sweeping switchbacks. The well-made path here consists of a staircase of stone slabs. These are followed down to a ford of the Red Burn and shortly afterwards the junction with the path to the Allt a'Mhuillin (c). Now it's just a case of following the outward route back to the Visitor Centre.

The North Face of Ben Nevis from the Carn Mor Dearg arete

FACT FILE

Tourist Information
Fort William Tourist Information Centre, Cameron Centre, Cameron Square, Fort William. Tel: 01397 703781. Open all year.
Ballachulish Information Centre, Car Park, Ballachulish. Tel: 01855 811296. Open Easter–October.
Spean Bridge Information Centre, Spean Bridge. Tel: 01397 712576. Open Easter–October.

Weather Forecasts
Knowing the weather forecast is useful in planning a day out. Although forecasts can be wrong – and we tend to remember the days when they are – they are far more accurate than in the past. The general forecasts carried on television and radio and in daily newspapers aren't specific enough for the walker. Much more useful are the outdoor forecasts for walkers and climbers on Radio Scotland at 6.55 p.m. on weekdays and 6.25 p.m. on Saturdays. The Scotsman newspaper also carries reports on hill conditions in its weather forecast though these aren't as up-to-date as the radio reports.

Outdoor shops in Fort William and Glen Coe display regular mountain weather forecasts from the Meteorological Office. These reports can be obtained as faxes or in spoken form from the following numbers. Be warned though, the charges are high.
Mountaincall West: 0891 500 441
Climbline West Highlands: 0891 654 669

Transport
The Ben Nevis and Glen Coe area is quite good for public transport. The West Highland Line runs through the area to Fort William and the latter is also a centre for many bus routes. This makes it possible to use public transport for many of the walks. Individual timetables are available for many companies but the most useful publication lists bus, train and ferry times in one volume called *Getting Round the Highlands and Islands*. This is edited by Peter R White and published by Southern Vectis, Nelson Road, Newport, Isle of Wight, PO30 1RD. Phone: 01983 522456. Fax: 01983 812983. Email: PWhite@argonet.co.uk

For local bus times contact Highland Country Buses: 01397 702373.
For Post Buses phone: 01463 256273.
For train times phone: 0345 484950.

Useful Addresses
Forestry Commission, Information, 231 Corstorphine Road, Edinburgh, EH12 7AT. Tel: 0131 334 0303.
John Muir Trust, 41 Commercial Street, Leith, Edinburgh, EH6 6JE. Tel: 0131 554 0114.
Mountain Bothies Association, General Secretary, 28 Duke Street, Clackmannan, FK10 4EF.
Mountaineering Council of Scotland, 4A St Catherine's Road, Perth, PH1 5SE. Tel: 01738 638 227.
National Trust for Scotland, 5 Charlotte Square, Edinburgh, EH2 4DU. Tel: 0131 226 5922.
Ramblers' Association Scotland. Tel: 01577 861222.
Ramblers' Association Head Office, 2nd Floor, Camelford House, 87–90 Albert Embankment, London SE1 7TW. Tel: 020 7339 8500.
Royal Society for the Protection of Birds, Scottish Headquarters, 17 Regent Terrace, Edinburgh, EH7 5BH.
Royal Society for the Protection of Birds, Head Office, The Lodge, Sandy, Bedfordshire, SG19 2DL.
Scottish Natural Heritage, 12 Hope Terrace, Edinburgh, EH9 2AS. Tel: 0131 554 9797.
Scottish Rights of Way Society, 10/2 Sunnyside, Edinburgh, EH7 5RA. Tel: 0131 652 2937.
Scottish Wild Land Group, Treasurer/Membership Secretary, 8 Cleveden Road, Kelvinside, Glasgow, G12 0NT.

Further Reading
Aitken, R., *The West Highland Way*, HMSO, 1990. Good guidebook with lots of interesting background information.
Bartholomew, J.C.; Bennet, D.J. & Stone, C., *Scottish Hill Tracks*, Scottish Rights of Way Society, 1995. Pocket guide to tracks through the hills.
Bearhop, D.A. (editor), *Munro's Tables*, SMT, 1997. Lists of summits including Corbetts and Grahams as well as Munros.

Bennet, Donald (editor), *The Munros*, SMT, 1985. Scottish Mountaineering Club Hillwalkers' Guide.

Brown, Hamish, *Pathfinder Guide: Fort William and Glen Coe Walks*, Jarrold Publishing/Ordnance Survey, 1996. Selection of 28 walks.

Brown, Hamish, *Hamish' Mountain Walk & Climbing the Corbetts*, Omnibus edition, Baton Wicks, 1997. Story of the first continuous walk over the Munros and a guide to the Corbetts.

Butterfield, Irvine, *The High Mountains of Britain and Ireland*, Diadem, 1986. Comprehensive guide to 3,000-foot peaks. Well-illustrated.

Crocket, Ken, *Ben Nevis*, SMT, 1986. History of the mountain.

Crumley, Jim, *Among Mountains*, Mainstream, 1993. Thoughtful and thought-provoking essays on the Highlands, including one on Glen Coe.

Darling, F. Fraser & Boyd, J. Morton, *The Highlands and Islands*, Collins New Naturalist, 1964. Classic natural history study.

Dempster, Andrew, *The Grahams: A Guide to Scotland's 2,000ft Peaks*, Mainstream, 1997. Illustrated guidebook.

Drummond, Peter, *Scottish Hill and Mountain Names*, SMT, 1991. Informative.

Gordon, Seton, *Highways and Byways in the West Highlands*, Birlinn, 1995. Classic guide first published in 1935.

Hodgkiss, Peter, *The Central Highlands*, SMT, 1994. Scottish Mountaineering Club District Guide.

Johnstone, Scott; Brown, Hamish; Bennet, Donald, Editors, *The Corbetts and Other Scottish Hills*, SMT, 1990. Scottish Mountaineering Club Hillwalkers Guide.

McNeish, Cameron, *The Munros: Scotland's Highest Mountains*, Lomond Books, 1996. Well-illustrated guide.

McNeish, Cameron, *The Munro Almanac & The Corbett Almanac*, Neil Wilson Publishing, 1996. Pocket size guides.

McOwan, Rennie, *The Man Who Bought Mountains*, NTS. Booklet on Percy Unna.

Moran, Martin, *Scotland's Winter Mountains*, David and Charles, 1988. Practical advice for the winter hillgoer.

Mountaineering Council of Scotland/Scottish Landowners' Federation (compilers), *Heading for the Scottish Hills*, SMT. Regular updates. Details of estates for stalking information.

Murray, W.H., *Scotland's Mountains*, SMT,

1987. Interesting introduction.

Murray, W.H., *Mountaineering in Scotland & Undiscovered Scotland*, Baton Wicks, 1998. Omnibus edition of two mountaineering classics first published in 1947 and 1951 respectively. Many of the adventures described take place on the Glen Coe and Ben Nevis hills.

Pringle, Ruaridh, *Hill Walks Glen Coe and Lochaber*, The Stationary Office, 1997. Useful guide to 20 hill walks.

Stott, Louis, *The Waterfalls of Scotland*, AUP, 1987. Comprehensive guide.

Thomson, Oliver and MacInnes, Hamish, *Glencoe*, NTS, 1994. Informative booklet from the National Trust for Scotland.

Tomkies, Mike, *A Last Wild Place*, Jonathan Cape, 1984. Natural history studies and adventures in the West Highlands

Townsend, Chris, *The Munros and Tops*, Mainstream, 1997. Story of the first continuous walk over all the 3,000' summits.

Townsend, Chris, *A Guide to Hillwalking*, Crowood, 1996. How to do it.

Townsend, Chris, *The Backpacker's Handbook*, Ragged Mountain Press, 1997. Comprehensive guide to camping and walking in wild country.

Williams, Noel, *Scrambles in Lochaber*, Cicerone, 1996. Pocket size guide.

Natural History Guides

Collins Pocket Guides:

Chinery, Michael, *Insects of Britain & Western Europe*, 1986.

Fitter, Richard; Fitter, Alastair and Blamey, Marjorie, *Wild Flowers of Britain and Northern Europe*, 1996.

Fitter, Richard; Fitter, Alastair and Farrer, Ann, *Grasses, Sedges, Rushes & Ferns of Britain and Northern Europe*, 1984.

Grey-Wilson, Christopher and Blamey, Marjorie, *Alpine Flowers of Britain and Europe*, 1995.

Heinzel, Hermann; Fitter, Richard and Parslow, John, *Birds of Britain & Europe*, 1995.

Mitchell, Alan and Wilkinson, John, *Trees of Britain & Northern Europe*, 1988.

All published by HarperCollinsPublishers.

Brown, R.W., Lawrence, M.J. and Pope, J, *Animal Tracks, Trails & Signs*, 1992, Hamlyn.

Sterry, Paul, Complete British Wildlife Photoguide, HarperCollinsPublishers, 1991.

Tolman, Tom and Lewington, Richard, Field Guide Butterflies of Britain and Europe, 1997, HarperCollinsPublishers.

How to use this book

This book contains route maps and descriptions for 30 walks. Each walk is graded (see p.3) and areas of interest are indicated by symbols (see below). For each walk particular points of interest are denoted by a capital letter both in the text and on the map (where the letter appears in a red box). In the text the route descriptions are prefixed by lower-case letters. We recommend that you read the whole description including the tinted box at the start of each walk before setting out.

Key to maps

P	Car park	—+—+—	Powerline
A	Campsite		Wide road (fenced, unfenced)
	Caravan site		Narrow road (fenced, unfenced)
	Youth hostel	— — — —	Track or forest road
	Public telephone	·-------	Footpath or old track
i	Information Point	-- -- ---	Intermittent path
	Mountain Rescue Post	·■ ▫ ᵘ ▫	Building, ruin or sheepfold

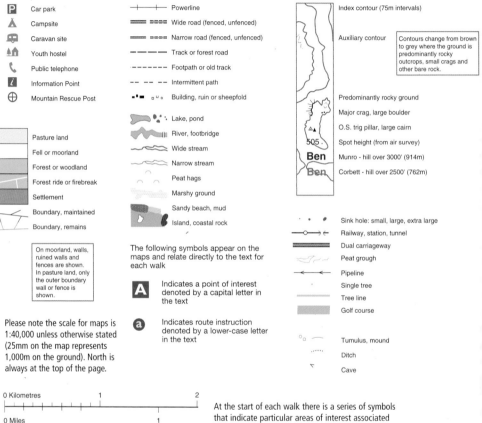

	Lake, pond
	River, footbridge
	Wide stream
	Narrow stream
	Peat hags
	Marshy ground
	Sandy beach, mud
	Island, coastal rock

Index contour (75m intervals)

Auxiliary contour

Contours change from brown to grey where the ground is predominantly rocky outcrops, small crags and other bare rock.

Predominantly rocky ground

Major crag, large boulder

O.S. trig pillar, large cairn

505 · Spot height (from air survey)

Ben Munro - hill over 3000' (914m)

Ben Corbett - hill over 2500' (762m)

	Pasture land
	Fell or moorland
	Forest or woodland
	Forest ride or firebreak
	Settlement
	Boundary, maintained
	Boundary, remains

On moorland, walls, ruined walls and fences are shown. In pasture land, only the outer boundary wall or fence is shown.

The following symbols appear on the maps and relate directly to the text for each walk

A Indicates a point of interest denoted by a capital letter in the text

a Indicates route instruction denoted by a lower-case letter in the text

Please note the scale for maps is 1:40,000 unless otherwise stated (25mm on the map represents 1,000m on the ground). North is always at the top of the page.

· • ● Sink hole: small, large, extra large

—○— ← Railway, station, tunnel

Dual carriageway

Peat ground

—◄—●—►— Pipeline

· Single tree

—— Tree line

Golf course

°₀ Tumulus, mound

.... Ditch

↳ Cave

0 Kilometres	1	2
0 Miles		1

At the start of each walk there is a series of symbols that indicate particular areas of interest associated with the route.

Key to symbols

The walks in this book are graded according to the level of difficulty, from easy to very difficult. We recommend that walks classified as difficult or very difficult (or moderate where indicated) should only be undertaken by experienced walkers who are competent in the use of map and compass and who are aware of the difficulties of the terrain they will encounter. The use of detailed maps is recommended for all routes.

Birdlife

Other wildlife

Wild flowers

Good views

Historical interest

Woodland